SOARING SPIRITS

SOARING SPIRITS

CONVERSATIONS WITH NATIVE AMERICAN TEENS

By Karen Gravelle

FRANKLIN WATTS
A Division of Grolier Publishing

The American Indian Experience
New York / London / Hong Kong / Sydney
Danbury, Connecticut

Jacket Photo: Lolita Black and Stanley Black, Quinault Indian Reservation
Frontis: Kristy and Fawn, Bay Mills Indian Reservation
Map by Gary S. Tong
All photographs by the author except for photo on page 91 supplied by
Loretta Cajero.

Library of Congress Cataloging-in-Publication Data

Gravelle, Karen.
    Soaring spirits: conversations with Native American teens/
by Karen Gravelle.
        p. cm.—(The American Indian experience)
    Includes bibliographical references (p. 123) and index.
    ISBN 0-531-11221-7
    1. Indian youth—United States—Social conditions. 2. Indian
youth—United States—Ethnic identity. 3. Indian youth—United
States—Social life and customs. I. Title. II. Series.
E98.Y68G73 1995
305.23'5—dc20   95-6822
                                                               CIP AC

◆◆◆

ACKNOWLEDGMENTS

In addition to the seventeen teenagers who participated in this book, I would like to thank the following adults— both for introducing their young people to me and for sharing their insights: Gloria LeBlanc, Carol McPherson, Debbie Lambert, Hilda Cree Garcia, Claudine Martinez, Juana and Joseph Pecos, Sherry Smith, and Josephine Smith. Thanks also to the Native American communities mentioned here for their warm hospitality and generosity.

Finally, a very special thanks to the young people of the Bay Mills Indian Reservation, who graciously allowed me to use the name of their youth group, Soaring Spirits, as the title of this book.

◆◆◆◆◆◆◆◆◆◆◆◆◆◆◆◆◆◆◆◆◆◆◆◆◆◆◆◆◆◆◆◆◆◆◆◆

CONTENTS

INTRODUCTION
9

1
CHEROKEE
13

2
SHINNECOCK
41

3
ANISHNABE
(OJIBWAY/CHIPPEWA)
51

4
QUINAULT
73

5
PUEBLO INDIANS
87

6
MOHAWK
105

**ATTENDING POWWOWS,
FEASTS, AND DANCES**
121

**FURTHER
READING**
123

INDEX
125

◆◆◆◆◆◆◆◆◆◆◆◆◆◆◆◆◆◆◆◆◆◆◆◆◆◆◆◆◆◆◆◆◆◆

INTRODUCTION

The 2 million Native Americans who currently live in the United States are proof that Indians are far from dead and gone.* Approximately one-half of these individuals make their homes on 300 federal and 21 state reservations. Most of the rest reside in cities such as New York, Buffalo, Tulsa, Phoenix, Chicago, Minneapolis, Seattle, Denver, Milwaukee, and Los Angeles.

Whether they live on a reservation or in a major metropolitan area, Native Americans tend to work at the same kinds of jobs as non-Native people in their area. For example, the parents of some of the young people in this book are employed as firefighters, schoolteachers, engineers, nurses, restaurant owners, government employees, artists, fishers, office workers, police officers, carpenters, and social workers.

Because Native Americans don't pitch tipis in their front yards or dress in buckskin and feathers, however, many non-Native people don't realize that they have Indians as their co-workers and neighbors. As a result, they frequently have little idea of how Native Americans live today, much less how they think and feel or what is important to them.

Like young people everywhere, Native American teens need to be seen for who they are and recognized for what they and their cultures have to offer. Thus, the teenagers who participated in this book wanted the

---

*Many Native people prefer the term Native American to the term Indian. Others object to both labels, feeling that neither one really fits. However, since the young people in this book used Native American and Indian interchangeably, both are used here.

chance to be heard and to share their ideas, hopes, and concerns with other kids their age.

The young people whose voices you'll hear in this book come from communities in the Northeast (the Shinnecock Reservation and the Akwesasne Mohawk Reservation in New York); the Southeast (the Cherokee Reservation in North Carolina); the Midwest (the Bay Mills Reservation in Michigan and the Roseau River Reservation in Manitoba); the Northwest (the Quinault Reservation in Washington); and the Southwest (Jemez Pueblo and the Pueblo of San Ildefonso in New Mexico).

As they are careful to say, they don't try to speak for all Native Americans, just for themselves. Although all live on reservations now, some have lived in cities and other non-Indian communities at one time or another. Thus, the experience of urban Indians is also represented here, at least partially.

While they have many different things to say, these young people agree on two points. They are all proud of their heritage as Native Americans and want others to understand the special things their cultures have to offer. But just as important, they want people to realize how much they have in common with everyone else.

POWWOWS AND DANCING

Since powwows, drumming, singing, and dancing are an important cultural and spiritual part of the lives of the teens in this book, we should understand what these activities are and what they mean to Native Americans.

Powwows are large gatherings of Native people that last several days. They are often held on a reservation, hosted by the particular tribe that lives there, but they may also be held in convention centers, public auditoriums, or stadiums. They are a chance for Indians of different nations to get to know each other, make new friends and visit with old ones, participate in cultural activities, sell their crafts, and generally have a good time. Because powwows are open to the general public as well, they are also an opportunity for non-Native people to meet Native Americans and to learn something about them and their culture.

Powwows are much more than this, however. The term *powwow* comes from the Algonquin word *pauwau*, originally used to describe medicine people and spiritual leaders. As this suggests, powwows are—in addition to everything else—religious events.

Singing, drumming, and dancing are a central part of powwows. For Native Americans, dances and the drumming and singing that accompany them are one way of praying, of honoring the Creator. Like teenagers from other ethnic groups, Native American teens enjoy dancing to popular music too. But dancing of that sort is done just for fun. While enjoyment is also part of Native American dancing, the primary purpose of these dances is spiritual, not recreational.

There are two types of Native American dancing. Traditional dancing is the older form. It's a slower style of dancing, with more dignified and more measured steps. There are many different traditional dances, such as the grass dance and the buffalo dance. The dress worn for traditional dancing depends on the meaning or theme of the dance.

Fancy dancing is a much newer dance form. As the name implies, fancy dancing is "fancier." The dancers move much faster, turning and twirling with their feet off the ground. In fancy dancing, the men wear two colorful feather bustles, one at the neck and the other on the back. Women fancy dancers wear shawls, which they us as part of the dance. Women also do the jingle dance, named for the jingling sound made by little bells sewn to their dresses.*

People of all ages—from very young children to elderly men and women—dance at powwows. In fact, one of the ways that children learn these dances is simply by joining in.

---

*You can see the top of a jingle dress on page 45.

◆◆◆◆◆◆◆◆◆◆◆◆◆◆◆◆◆◆◆◆◆◆◆◆◆◆◆◆◆◆◆◆◆◆

1
CHEROKEE

When the Spanish explorer Hernando de Soto entered the Great Smoky Mountains in 1540, he found a nation of 25,000 Cherokees controlling a vast area of what would later beome the southeastern United States. At that time, the Cherokees' territory covered more than 135,000 square miles, encompassing parts of Virginia, Kentucky, North Carolina, South Carolina, Tennessee, Georgia, and Alabama.

Over the next three centuries, the Cherokee, like other Native people in the East, lost more and more of their land to European settlers. Finally, in 1837, President Andrew Jackson (whose life, ironically, had been saved by a Cherokee chief) ordered the Cherokee to be rounded up and moved to land in Oklahoma, in an action that has come to be called the Removal. During the next year and a half, 16,000 Cherokee were marched over 1,200 miles to their new "home" across the Mississippi. Four thousand men, women, and children died on this trip, a journey the Cherokee call the Trail of Tears.

The effort to rid the Southeast of the Cherokee people was not completely successful, however. By hiding in the mountains, some managed to escape the Removal. Today, their descendants form the Eastern Band of the Cherokee Nation. (The Western Band is composed of those living in Oklahoma.) Of the 10,400 people who make up the Eastern Band, 7,800—including Shondi, Matthew, Emerson, Winnie, and Skooter—live on the Qualla Boundary, the 56,000-acre Cherokee Reservation in the mountains of western North Carolina.

CHEROKEE RESERVATION
(QUALLA BOUNDARY)
CHEROKEE, NORTH CAROLINA

I meet people—tourists sometimes—who come up here and say, "Where's the tipis and the horses?" Once, when I was down at the Tee Pee Restaurant with my friends, one bunch came in and they said, "Where's the reservation?" We said, "You're standing on it."

—Winnie

I went to a college recruitment visit to Duke this winter and one of the boys in the dorm where I was staying said, "Where are you from?" And I said, "Cherokee, North Carolina." And he goes, "I'm from Alabama, and I come up through Cherokee on my way to school and I didn't see a single Cherokee Indian!" I said, "Maybe you didn't know what you were looking for." And he said, "Well, I looked pretty hard!" I just wanted to tell him, "They were probably all at work."

—Matthew

Situated in the Great Smoky Mountains, the Cherokee Reservation is an unusually beautiful place. Often touched by a blue mist that gives them their name, the

Smoky Mountains have an enchanted, otherworldly quality. The forested hillsides, sparkling waterfalls, and trout-filled streams attract thousands of vacationers each year to Cherokee and to the national park that borders it on the north.

Shondi, Emerson, and Matthew have lived on the reservation all their lives. While Skooter and Winnie were born in Cherokee, they have also lived in other places. Neither of them liked these places much.

"I moved around the eastern coast a lot," Skooter says. "I've been in Virginia, Kentucky, Tennessee. My father used to be in underground construction, so for my first six years of elementary school, I bounced around a lot. It was rough at times," he adds, "being the one little Indian kid in the school."

"I was born here, but when I was nine years old, my mom and my dad had a divorce, so we moved to South Carolina. We moved back two years ago," Winnie states. "I was homesick. I didn't blend in with all the other people. I missed the mountains and I missed all my friends."

Although tourists visit Cherokee all the time, as a child, Winnie had no contact with them. Thus, Spartanburg, South Carolina, came as a bit of a culture shock. "The first time I'd seen different races besides Indians was down there. There were white people and black people, Chinese."

Since none of the Spartansburg children had ever seen an Indian before, Winnie was as much of an oddity to them as they were to her. "The first day there, I went to school and all these kids said, 'Are you Chinese?'"

Although non–Native Americans have had contact with the Cherokee for over 500 years, most—including many who claim to have distant Cherokee ancestry—seem to think that the Cherokee people have all died out. As Matthew says, "I think that a lot of people who

Winnie Jumper, age 15

don't live around us—white people—I'm not sure that they know we still exist. To them, Indians are just somebody in a history book."

Even the people who are aware that there is a Cherokee Reservation in North Carolina often have rather strange ideas as to what Indians should be like. "I've noticed that people will come in and be amazed that we don't live in tipis," Skooter says. "They come in, and they say, 'Where's the Indians? Where's the reservation?'

"I was eating at Burger King about two weeks ago, and two little kids were with their mother, and she's sitting in Burger King, right dead center of the reservation, downtown. The kids were jumping up and down —they were getting bored and cranky, going, 'Can't we do something?' And she said, 'Well, in just a minute, we're going to leave, and your dad's going to find the Indian reservation around here somewhere. And we're going to find some Indians.' I thought that was kind of funny."

Not only do others expect Cherokee people to live very differently, but they also have misconceptions as to what they should look like. Frequently, Cherokees are not recognized as being Native people by the very tourists who have come to see them. Although this can be annoying, most, like Matthew and his friends, try to handle it with humor.

"I was sitting on the bridge in town with one of my friends," he recalls. "And this person stopped in the middle of the bridge and asked my friend, and my friend looks a lot more Indian than me, 'Where are all the Indians at around here?' And my friend said, 'There haven't been any Indians around here since the Removal. They all went to Oklahoma.' And the guy goes, 'Damn!' He got mad and left. He didn't get mad at my friend's joking. He took him seriously."

Matthew Bradley, age 17

Aside from their ignorance about Indians and the way in which they live, non–Native Americans may have difficulty recognizing Cherokees as Indians because many Cherokee resemble other people living in the area. Cherokees have had close contact with other groups for centuries and during that time have often intermarried with them.

"It's a different thing for us than other Indians where the blood lines are more purebred," Matthew explains. "We have a lot of people with white and Indian parentage. There are hardly any full-blooded Cherokee, so we have people with Indian features or darker skin and others like me who hardly look Indian at all."

Each tribe has the legal right to define its criteria for tribal enrollment, or membership. Thus, like other Indian nations, the Cherokee determine for themselves who has enough Cherokee ancestry to be considered a Cherokee. The Eastern Band requires that a person be one-sixteenth Cherokee to be enrolled. The Western Band has more lenient criteria. They require only that a person have an ancestor who was enrolled.

Recently, the Eastern Band considered making it easier for people to qualify for enrollment. "This past year, we had a big controversy at the tribal council," Skooter says. "See, you have to be at least one-sixteenth to be on the Eastern Band roll, to qualify for the hospital and things like that. They were thinking about dropping it to one thirty-second. That'd be another whole division down."

The reason for considering this was that many people who have some Cherokee blood and have lived and worked in the community can't qualify for enrollment and the privileges awarded to Indians, such as being qualified to hold tribal land in their names or benefiting from preferential hiring for jobs. "Like the coach here, he doesn't qualify. But he grew up here all his life, he went to school here, played all the sports here, and he works here now, but he never had the opportunity to be considered a Cherokee," Skooter explains.

"It went on for two to three months," he continues. "It was real big. The whole reservation voted on it." In the end, they decided against the proposal.

"The tribe voted against it because they feel that too many people are just saying that they're Indians," Shondi comments. "Most people think you should have to be at least half Indian to get on the roll."

Shondi acknowledges that it's not a simple issue, though. "I think it should be half. But then a lot of people here who don't have that much still really take pride in our culture."

"It's hard for people who have a lot [of Cherokee blood] to understand what the others are going through," Skooter adds. "People just didn't feel that they wanted the whites moving in; they don't want to be diluted down. That's pretty much the deal.

"To me, it doesn't matter what else you have in you, as long as you do have the Indian blood. But for some that are lying just to get the acceptance or the fringe benefits, that *does* bother me," he says. "That angers me!"

Winnie, Emerson, Matthew, Shondi, and Skooter have varying degrees of Cherokee ancestry. Emerson's father is a full-blooded Cherokee, and Emerson is three-fourths Cherokee. Although Matthew's mother is Cherokee, his father is white.

Shondi knows her heritage down to the last decimal point. "I'm 57.81 percent Cherokee," she says. "I went recently to get my Indian papers for a job, and I noticed it when they were looking up my name."

"I'm not quite half, but I qualify," Skooter says. My mother's three-quarters Cherokee, but my dad's mother, she's white. That cut him way below half. He's on the roll, but I'd say he's one-sixteenth."

Regardless of the amount of Cherokee ancestry they have, all five of these young people are proud of their heritage and, in one way or another, help to keep their culture alive.

Shondi likes going to powwows, although she doesn't dance herself. "There aren't too many kids at our school who dance," she says. "I wish that I did. I think when you watch them and realize what they're doing, then you have a yearning to be with them."

Even so, she gets a lot out of just observing. "You feel proud to watch other kids your age get out there and dance," she says.

"I also feel proud about how Sequoya made our alphabet," Shondi continues. In 1821, the Cherokee became the first Native people in North America to have a written language. Using an alphabet invented by the Cherokee scholar Sequoya, they began publishing their own newspaper in 1828.* Today, this alphabet is still in use and all Cherokee children learn to read and write it in school.

"In the elementary school, they have a class and they're starting to write cartoons in Indian for our reservation newspaper. We just had a big snow, and they wrote stories about it in Cherokee and put them in the paper," Shondi adds.

Emerson follows a long Cherokee artistic tradition. In addition to his own drawings, paintings, and carvings, he takes great pride in his grandmother's artistic accomplishments. The Cherokee are famous for their beautiful and complex basketwork, and many of the Eastern Band support themselves by selling baskets and other works of art. "My grandma, I think she's the best

---

*Some of Sequoya's descendants, such as Skooter's family on his mother's side, still live in Cherokee.

basket maker in Cherokee," he says proudly. "She made fifteen hundred dollars from one basket."

Winnie is one of the few young people in the Eastern Band who dance at powwows. "I learned from my grandpa and grandma," she says. "They've got two different ways you can dance. You can dance fancy or traditionally."

Like Shondi, Winnie takes pride in the Cherokee language. Although she doesn't speak it fluently, she can understand it. "When my grandma talks to me in Indian—she does it all the time —I can understand what she's saying, but I can't talk it. We have to take Cherokee history, learn our culture, and how to talk in Indian to graduate high school, but we talk different. The way they speak now is different from the way my grandmother says it. They pronounce it in a different way," Winnie explains.

Her grandmother is also an important source of information about Indian medicine. "I was sick a few weeks ago," Winnie recalls. "And my grandma went out and got some bark off a cherry tree, and she dug up some yellow root and boiled it and made me drink it. It doesn't taste good, but it helps."

For Winnie, Cherokee legends are also an important part of her culture. "There's one about how the turtle got lines in its shell. I can't remember all of it, but he did something bad, and he fell off a cliff for his punishment. He was broken all into pieces. He asked God to help him live again, but he had to have those lines in his shell and couldn't be pretty anymore."

Legends and storytelling interest Skooter as well. "We have local people teaching the tales and stories, local people producing books and reading them. They all teach a moral somehow. It's something to look back onto, to help keep in touch," he states.

He enjoys helping pass these tales on to the younger

generation. "My little sister and brother are just four and two now. They're at the age when everything excites them! Little kids all the time want to hear about Spear Finger,* and I like to tell them stuff like that. The story might vary, but Spear Finger eats the livers of people. She can shape-shift—she might be a real old woman or a beautiful young girl. It's very popular here!"

Skooter also likes to write stories himself. Recently he helped his mother explore and preserve some of the beliefs of older Cherokees.

"I don't know if you've ever heard tell about the Little People," he says. "Most people think it's a legend, but a lot of people stand by it. My mother, she attends Western Carolina University, and she had to do a big write-up about the Little People. I helped her out a little bit.

"We went out to see some of the elder people of the reservation. A lot of people wouldn't talk to us. I think it's something they think just shouldn't be talked about a lot, or they may get criticized for believing in them. But some were very helpful.

"Anyhow, the Little People are tiny little people—Indians—who are mischievous and go around doing things. I have heard people talk about being at home or something, when a dish falls and breaks and you hear a little giggle, and you see something running by. It's not your cat and it's not your dog. . . .

"Some people claim to be kind of masters, and have them—I don't want to say as pets—but take care of them. It's kind of spooky," he adds, "but I'd like to write more about them."

---

*Spear Finger is a legendary evil spirit capable of taking human or animal shapes. In these disguises, Spear Finger preys on people, killing them and cutting their bodies open with its clawlike spear finger.

Skooter McCoy, age 17

In addition to the classes he takes in school, Matthew seeks out other information about his heritage. "There's a class here, and we get to learn some. But I've always been interested in it myself—it's the kind of thing I study on my own," he says.

Recently he's begun reading work by Native American authors. In a summer class at the University of North Carolina, he was introduced to some poetry by N. Scott Momaday, a Kiowa writer. "He was real good!" Matthew says enthusiastically. "I was surprised that there are so many Indians who like to write. Really, that's something that I'd like to see more of!"

Staying connected with their culture isn't always easy for Cherokee teenagers, however. "We have lost a lot of tradition. We've lost a lot of . . . everything!" Skooter says. "The elders, they try to teach us the ways and try to keep it intact so we can pass it on to our children and it won't die out one day.

"But it's very hard. I mean MTV and television—we see what they're doing and we want to do that—their styles, the different types of music. It's hard to maintain what's important to you. A lot of the kids, sometimes they get tired of it. Everybody else is moving along, changing with the times. Sometimes they're kind of left behind with the old ways."

He feels it's even harder for kids who come from more mixed backgrounds. "It's really about how you grow up at home, I believe," Skooter continues. "Some parents are strong on tradition and teach the kids the Indian dances, the language, just the ways of the Indian.

"I have a lot of white people in my family; I'm not as in tune to the Indian ways. Now, my grandparents on my mother's side, they're full-blooded. And anytime I have a question or need help, I can go to see them. But there are times that I wish I had more input and understood more about my ancestors."

Even attending cultural events isn't quite the same for him as for others who have more Native American ancestry. Occasionally he has overheard comments at powwows that suggest he isn't completely accepted.

"Sometimes you do feel uncomfortable," Skooter says. "I've been to a few powwows. I'm not a dancer, but I like to go and watch. I have a lighter skin tone than most and I don't have the real jet black, long hair. My brother and sister have blue eyes and sandy-blond hair. Sometimes, you feel like you don't fit in there. I know a couple of times I've heard comments when people are dancing. You know, 'That's a five-dollar Indian,' or whatever. Because there are some light-complexioned people who do dance. It does hurt sometimes," he admits.

Of the five, Winnie is the only one who feels comfortable with the idea of perhaps marrying someone who isn't a Native person. Emerson and Shondi both seem to just assume that they will choose to marry another Indian when they decide to settle down. But because their backgrounds are more mixed, the issue has different ramifications for Matthew and Skooter.

"I don't think I'd ever marry a white girl," Matthew says, although this isn't because he dislikes whites or thinks there's something wrong with them. It's just that he has experienced difficulty because of his own mixed background. "I've never liked having a white father, looking white like I do," he explains. " I wouldn't want to have a baby that felt the same way."

"Ideally, I'd like to marry an Indian girl, but if it wasn't another Indian, I'd like to marry another minority person," Matthew continues. "It would kind of worry me if I met a girl that was white who I might want to marry. I don't know how I'd deal with that, so I really don't get too involved with white girls."

Skooter is concerned about his children being eligible

to be enrolled as Cherokees. "I thought about it," he says. "If I was to marry somebody who's white, that would hurt my children along the line. I would probably like to marry somebody of the Cherokee, to keep my blood-line for my children, so they can have all that I've got—government recognition as an enrolled member of the Eastern Band of the Cherokee Indians, the great school here, the health services, and the ability to hold tribal land in my name. I want my children to hang on to their heritage and what it means to be a Cherokee."

Like all of the young people in this book, Cherokees are acutely sensitive to the negative manner in which they have been portrayed in movies, television, and history books. Thus, recent films, such as *Dances with Wolves*, have been a welcome change.

"I love the lastest movies! *Dances with Wolves*, stuff like that, was great!" Skooter says enthusiastically. "We're finally not being seen as the bad guys. We're not the sneaky people who jumped on the covered wagons. We had intelligence—it shows in these films! *The Last of the Mohicans, Thunderheart*—we've enjoyed them, everyone around here has!"

Some people from Cherokee were actually involved in making *The Last of the Mohicans*. Although the story takes place in New York State, the movie was actually filmed in the Smoky Mountains. "A bunch of people here were in that movie," Winnie says. "Two of my cousins were in it, and they liked it."

Still, seeing the movie and being reminded of the things that happened to Native people were upsetting for her. "It kind of made me mad at first," she says. "When you think about it, we were here first and every-thing. They shouldn't have treated Indians like they did. To think that there was a bunch of us at one time, and now there's not that many."

The issue of how they are portrayed to others takes

on an additional twist for the Cherokee because they have an ongoing theater production in their midst that is presumably based on their history. The Trail of Tears inspired a play called *Unto These Hills* that tells of the Eastern Band's success in refusing to be removed from the Great Smoky Mountains. The play is performed during the summer in an open-air theater on the reservation and, since it first opened in 1950, has attracted thousands of tourists to the area.

Although the playwright and the majority of actors are not Cherokee, nevertheless, in one way or another, *Unto These Hills* affects the lives of most of the people living on the reservation. Most important is the play's economic impact. As Matthew puts it, "It's a big money-maker! It attracts tourists, who spend their money in other places."

In addition to attracting tourist dollars, *Unto These Hills* is a major employer. "Quite a few people here work there. It's mainly the younger generation—the high school students, the elementary kids," says Skooter. "They get jobs for the crowd scenes."

Emerson is a strong supporter of *Unto These Hills*. "I like it!" he exclaims. He's also one of the few Cherokees who have a major role in the play. "I worked there for two years," Emerson continues. "This will be my third year. I've been playing a principal for two years, a council chief. I'm in the crowd scenes, too."

Matthew's family is also very involved in the production, but not as actors. "The large majority of their employees are Indians. My mother works up there. She's a nurse, the company nurse. My uncle—the man that married my aunt, he's white—he's the general manager of the drama. And I work there," he says.

"Plus, they put back into the community. You can apply for scholarships. They give a lot of money out for kids to go to college."

Emerson Welch, age 15

The economic benefits aren't the only good thing about the drama. By attracting non-Native people to Cherokee, *Unto These Hills* makes other Americans aware that the Cherokee people still exist and educates them about the Removal. "I like people to know what happened," says Skooter. "We were a really big nation here at one time. We occupied Tennessee, Kentucky, Virginia, North Carolina, Georgia, South Carolina. I would like people to know more about that."

Nevertheless, it's strange to see white people playing most of the major Indian roles. "It's just like all those old movies on TV with people in paint," Winnie says. As she explains, though, "They have tryouts for the parts, but not many people try out. Most of the people around here are usually in the crowd scenes."

Matthew agrees. "Some people say, 'Why are these white people playing Indians?' But see, there aren't a lot of Indian actors. It would be great if all Indians played Indians, but it's not really possible. I don't think anyone wants to see the drama go away because there's a lack of Indian actors," he adds.

But they do wish the white actors wouldn't make mistakes that are easily correctable. "They speak the language differently," Emerson says. "They say the words incorrectly from the way they're supposed to be pronounced."

"It is—I'm not going to say it's offending—but it does bother me that a lot of it's changed," Skooter adds. "I mean the simple pronunciation of words. Some of the names have been changed around. They're not pronounced the right way. And when you do it the wrong way, it means something totally different in the language we've got here."

Also, the play is not totally accurate, perhaps because it wasn't written by a Cherokee. "It's not as authentic as people think," Skooter continues. "The story line pretty much is the truth, but some of the elder people around say the stuff they portray really didn't happen that way.

"The actors don't take the time, I don't think. Sometimes, I don't believe they really understand what went on. They haven't studied what it was about. They do a fine job, but I would like to see people who know more about it portraying how they feel it really was."

Despite the generally good feelings about the drama and the economic benefits it brings, there is another, more negative, side to tourism. As Matthew points out, "A lot of the places tourists spend their money . . . well, they employ Native Americans in the minimum-wage jobs, but the businesses are owned by people who aren't Indian. We're so dependent on tourism here, and it's such a seasonal industry," he adds. "It leaves a lot of unemployment in the winter. I wish that we could have more industry, other kinds of jobs as well."

During the school year, when the drama is closed and the tourists are gone, sports are the major nonacademic activity for most students. The girls at Cherokee play softball, basketball, volleyball, and some golf. But, as is true throughout the country, the emphasis is on the boys' teams.

Skooter is a promising football player in his junior year and hopes to get a college scholarship playing ball. As a sophomore football player, Emerson expects to be part of Cherokee High School's most successful team. "We're the best Cherokee's ever had," he states proudly. "See, JV had never won the Smoky Mountain Conference. And last year, they won the conference undefeated, beating the other teams by forty to fifty points!"

Matthew is also very involved in sports, but in a somewhat unconventional manner. He runs track and cross-country, an activity not many Cherokee kids participate in. "Track is the activity in my life that I enjoy the most," he says. "It's something that I'm dedicated to and spend a lot of practice time on.

"But I find among my peers, people don't understand it; some might think I'm foolish for spending all the time I do on what I do. Younger and older people, they really admire it, but people my own age, they consider it more as an oddity."

There was a reason he chose track. "When I was younger, I played everything—baseball, soccer, football, basketball—but I was never really good at it," Matthew explains. "But when I was thirteen, I started running track. That's what I'm really good at. If I had my choice, I'd probably play basketball or some spectator sport, but I have lofty goals and I saw that track was the only sport I could achieve anything in."

Sports also provide one of the few opportunities for Cherokees of the Eastern Band to associate with kids from the Western Band. "Twice a year, we have what is known as NAYO [Native American Youth Organization] sports. All the Indian tribes in America come together at the same time," Skooter explains.

"The Western Cherokee teams come in. And it's amazing! A lot of times, you will see someone you think could be your brother or your sister—they just look so much like you! Down the road somewhere, you must have had the same grandpa.

"It's nice when they come in. We talk and we go out and eat together and play ball against each other. But that happens over Easter weekend and then one weekend in the summer, and that's really all. And it's just for the athletes, not all the kids. But it's better than nothing, I guess," he adds.

Although Shondi, Emerson, Matthew, Skooter, and Winnie all live on the reservation, they have contact with neighboring white children. Cherokee children can

Shondi Johnson, age 16

go either to local public schools, which are primarily white, or to schools on the reservation.

When she was younger, Shondi attended a public elementary school. It was OK, but, as she explains, "I like this school better. I just feel more at home here than I do somewhere else."

One of the reasons Cherokee feel more comfortable going to their own school is the attitude of some white youngsters. "Basically, we're accepted most of the places we go," Winnie states, "but sometimes people get to teasing us—saying 'most of the Indians are just drunks,' and stuff. I mean, *some* of us are, but not all of us."

Emerson agrees. "White people make fun of us," he says. "At football games, they'll be hollering, putting their hands on their mouths, going, 'Woo, woo.' The tomahawk chop stuff." Emerson thinks they know this bothers him and other Cherokees, and that that is why they do it. "Every time we play against each other, there's a fight or something, on the court or on the field. It's like they're out for blood."

Few Cherokee teenagers choose to go to public high schools. "Most of the kids reject that," Skooter says. "It's sort of a form of being a traitor, leaving."

Matthew actually went to public high school for a while, but didn't like it much. "It's where my mom wanted me to go," he explains, "but I didn't care for it. People there thought the people here were inferior.

"A big thing at the high school I went to was athletics—to be able to beat Cherokee High School. A lot of people like to compete hard against Cherokee, but at that school, they base a lot of their success on that. It makes them feel better about themselves or something.

"Not that I so much minded competing with the kids here," Matthew continues. "I just didn't want to be associated with that attitude."

He's glad he transferred to Cherokee High School. "I came here February of my freshman year," he recalls. "People were a lot more friendly to me here than at the public school. I met more people here the first day of school than I met there the whole semester."

Not only do Cherokees sometimes attend white schools, but some white kids who live in the area go to Cherokee High. "A lot of times, most times, it works out," Skooter says. "It's great! Everybody gets along. But I'm not going to tell you there's never been a racial slander or a 'white kid' or 'white trash' or anything like that. It happens."

He has observed, however, that the white kids who come usually don't stay. "A lot of times, families move into the area, stop for a while, and then move back out." But he doesn't think that's the whole reason. "I notice a lot of times kids do not stay through all of high school. I don't know if it's what we've done or anything that's run them off, but sometimes they have trouble fitting in here, like I would in a white public school. You need your type around you a lot of times to fit in."

Matthew thinks part of the problem between white kids and Cherokee people is that some whites resent the economic entitlements that the government provides to the Cherokee. "You know, western North Carolina is not a rich place. It's one of the poorest places in the nation," he explains. "So, we get used as a scapegoat, I guess.

"We do get a lot of help from the government. But they think if we want to buy a car or something, we ask the BIA [Bureau of Indian Affairs] for money and we'll get it. It doesn't work quite that way."

Jealousy around this issue sometimes surfaces over seemingly minor things. "I've still got some friends at the public high school I went to," Matthew says. "One time I went to an event at a community college, and I was sitting with these friends. We [Cherokees] have a boys' club, and we always travel on charter buses, which is cool. And they said, 'How did y'all get up here?' I said, 'We took a charter.' They said, 'The Braves always travel in class, don't they?' And this other boy sitting across from us said, 'They *travel* in class—they don't *have* any class. They just have more money than us.'"

Unlike most kids from Cherokee, Winnie, Shondi, Emerson, Skooter, and Matthew all plan to go on to college when they graduate. "Not many people around here go to college. They drop out of school and not many of them even graduate," Winnie states. "But I want to go on to college and get a career, so at least some of us can!"

Shondi agrees. "Not too many people at all go to school," she says, "But I'm going to go, because I don't want to be like everybody else!"

The two girls have very different plans for the future, however. "I like kids, so I'd like to be a pediatrician," Shondi says. Although she doesn't plan to live on the reservation all her life, Shondi doesn't like to think too much about what she'll do after high school. "It's scary!" she admits. "My friends and I—we don't talk about it that much—we don't want to graduate!"

Right now, Winnie is undecided as to whether she wants to be a corporate lawyer or a journalist. "I've always been fascinated by law," she explains. "My cousins are cops, and I always liked listening to them tell about their work. But my parents won't let me be a cop, so I want to be a lawyer."

On the other hand, since she also likes to write, Winnie thinks that maybe she'd like to be a reporter or a TV journalist. She's always wanted to go to the University of North Carolina, but after that she expects to return, if not to the reservation itself, at least to the general area.

Although he plans to go to junior college to major in art, Emerson definitely plans to come back to the reservation. "People think they can move away from Cherokee," he says. "But they can't, because they can't live without mountains."

"I'll probably get a degree in some kind of health occupation," Skooter says. "Physical therapy, stuff like that. Some of my family's in that, and I want to help people. You get a reward just going to work every day," he adds. "I'd really like to work in a profession like that."

He's not sure exactly where he'll go after college, though. "It's hard to say. A lot of times, people go away. They experience the world, you know, and sometimes they don't want to come back. But sometimes they get out there and it doesn't work out the way they'd planned or dreamed of, and they do come back. It's home, it's a place to come back to.

"For myself, though, I don't see myself coming back here right away. I'm a southern boy, so I think I'll end up back here someday, but I don't actually see myself coming back to the reservation to work."

"I have a desire now to move away, see the rest of the world," says Matthew, and he's applied to colleges as far away as Florida. "There are two things I'd be interested in—journalism, because people are always saying I'm a good writer, and Asian studies. I don't know if I want to pursue a career in that, but it's something I want to study to *see* if I want to."

Regardless of whether they intend to return or want to try life outside of Cherokee, Winnie, Emerson, Matthew, Shondi, and Skooter all feel the reservation has been a good place to grow up. "I think the best thing for me was being around a lot of Indian kids here—it's easier," Skooter says. "But when you're off—like for me, when my family was traveling around—it's difficult because you may not be understood. You can't sit down and tell somebody something you want to tell them because they're not really going to understand.

"No matter what I do, or go off, or whatever happens, I can always come back here and belong here. It's one big, huge family. That's good! It's like security, you know."

For Skooter, the reservation symbolizes a circle, an important concept in all Native American cultures. "A group of people is like a circle—you're all connected, you hold trust," he explains. "If one breaks away or does something to hurt the rest of the circle, it's a broken circle. And it makes the whole group weaker."

Like every place, however, Cherokee has both good and bad points. "It's fifty-fifty," explains Matthew. "There's a lot of good things! In one way, there's a lot of support for you. Things we do are a lot slower—the kids are more conservative, I guess, quieter. It's harder to entice your friends to do something you're not supposed to do. In some ways, it gets boring, but at least you can be grateful that it's quiet. The good thing about the reservation is it keeps Indian people together and gives them a chance to succeed.

"But the bad things are that it's a small, boring place, and everybody always does the same thing, and not a lot of people want to leave the reservation. And there's more drinking and drug use here than in communities around us, and that's bad."

Matthew also thinks it's hard for people who are different or who have different aspirations. "I'm a lot different from a lot of kids, not just in the way I look, but in the way I act. And a lot of people stand back from me.

"I've heard people say, 'Indians are always trying to keep other Indians back.' In some cases, that's true—people who want to get ahead get looked at a different way.

"It's kind of necessary to have a reservation so Indian people can stay together in an Indian community," he continues. "But, in a way, I think it's better, if you want, to go out into the mainstream and see what's going on."

In spite of where he ends up, however, Matthew concludes, "There's good and bad things about being an Indian, but there's no race I'd rather be associated with."

◆◆◆◆◆◆◆◆◆◆◆◆◆◆◆◆◆◆◆◆◆◆◆◆◆◆◆◆◆◆◆◆◆◆◆◆

2
SHINNECOCK

Since books mention the Shinnecock only briefly, if at all, most information about them must be obtained from Shinnecocks themselves. As someone who has lived on the Shinnecock Reservation all her life, Aiyana knows as much about their history as anyone. "At the time of the first European contact in 1640, the Shinnecock territory stretched sixty miles along the south shore of Long Island, from present-day Moriches to East Hampton," she says.

As a coastal people, the Shinnecock depended primarily on the sea for their livelihood, relying particularly on shellfish. To supplement their diet, they hunted rabbits, ducks, and geese, and gathered wild nuts, berries, fruits, and vegetables.

Like other Algonquin tribes of the Northeast, they lived in wigwams—dome-shaped homes made of poles covered with bark, animal skins, or woven mats. These wigwams could be seen among the Shinnecock as late as the 1850s. They also used the trees and grasses around them for weaving baskets, a skill that has been preserved by a few elderly members of the community.

The Shinnecock were never a large group, even before the coming of Europeans. Today, 350 to 400 Shinnecock live on an 800-acre peninsula in the Shinnecock Bay. This land, together with an additional 100 acres nearby, comprises the Shinnecock Reservation. Like their ancestors, many Shinnecock still make a living from shellfish. Their Presbyterian church, which forms the center of much of reservation community life, is the oldest missionary church in the United States.

SHINNECOCK RESERVATION
SOUTHAMPTON, NEW YORK

You just need to go back to your roots and learn about yourself first. And then once you learn about yourself and have good self esteem, then you'll be able to learn about other people.

—Aiyana

The Shinnecock Reservation differs in a number of ways from the other Native American communities presented in this book. First, it's the most eastern, with only the Atlantic Ocean standing between it and the continent of Europe. Just two hours away from the center of New York City, it is also the closest to a major metropolitan area. Finally, it is probably the only Indian reservation in the country that is situated in the middle of a vacation spot for the rich and famous. Million-dollar estates are not uncommon in the neighboring towns of Southampton and Amagansett, and each summer the surrounding area becomes the temporary home of wealthy writers, well-known rock stars, and famous actors.

Although eastern Long Island has little in common with the mountains of western North Carolina, the Cherokee and the Shinnecock are similar in having had to face particularly difficult—although different—obstacles in holding on to their identity.

In a state where the few Native people are clustered in the north and the west, the Shinnecock are a small group isolated in the far east. Thus, in the past, many Shinnecock rarely saw any Indian people but themselves. Fortunately, contact with other groups has increased recently, and this is changing how the young people of Shinnecock view themselves.

Aiyana had a head start in maintaining her heritage because both her parents are firmly rooted in their culture. Some of the other kids have had a harder time staying connected to their Native American traditions. "Before, there were not many who were really interested in their culture. But in the last five years, a lot more kids are becoming interested," Aiyana says. "More kids started going to powwows and to see things. Then they'd come back to the res [reservation] and be more interested in their heritage. And then others would connect with these kids and say, 'Hey, I'm Indian too and I want to know about that, too.'"

Although the Shinnecock are becoming more involved in their culture, they have an uphill battle getting others to see them as Indians. As a nation, they are virtually never mentioned in books on Native Americans, except perhaps as one of the long-extinct tribes of the East Coast. Many of their neighbors on the eastern half of Long Island—to say nothing of people in the rest of the country—are unaware that they even exist.

Like the Cherokee, the Shinnecock often don't look the way others think Indians should look, and this further complicates matters. In the case of the Shinnecock, however, many have some African-American ancestry and, as a result, are assumed by non–Native Americans

Aiyana Smith, age 17

to be black. Even when it's known that they are from the reservation, Shinnecock teenagers with visible African ancestry are often pressured by black kids to identify themselves as blacks, not as Indians.

In the ethnic dynamics of her school, "we're always kind of stuck in the middle," Aiyana states. Southampton High School is predominantly white, with a minority of African-American, Hispanic, and approximately thirty Shinnecock students. "The past year, there was a lot of racial tension all over Long Island," Aiyana recalls. "It was basically the blacks against the whites, or the blacks and Hispanics against the whites."

The Shinnecock students sympathized with the black students' position and wanted to support them. But they wanted to do this on their own terms, something the black students had difficulty understanding.

"The black kids wanted us to join with them but they didn't want us to keep our own identity," Aiyana says. "They were saying, 'It doesn't matter if you're Indian or black, you're still black.' They didn't want to accept the fact that we were Native.

"All the Native students felt really pressured!" she continues. "The black students couldn't understand that it wasn't anything we had against black people—it was just that we're Native, not black.

"It was a big issue—kids were ready to fight over it! After a lot of meetings, we got our point across, though. They understood where we were coming from and we got to understand where they were coming from."

Although non–Native kids may think the Shinnecock teenagers seem indistinguishable from the rest of the minority student body, Aiyana feels there are aspects of life on the reservation that make her people distinctly Indian. "A lot of our people are really close to nature," she says.

"For example, my grandmother is very knowledgeable about plants—the different plants we use for medicines. We make cough medicine from cherry bark and make blackberry tea for stomach pains. They really work!" she adds.

"We still make teas from natural plants like sumac and wintergreen. We eat some of the natural foods, like pokeweed. You have to get them before the shoots are mature, because when they're bigger, they're poisonous. And we still go out and get berries. The kids play in the woods and pick berries and bring them home to their families or give them to the elders."

Basketweaving may be dying out but other crafts, such as making scrubs, are still alive. Scrubs are sturdy brushes made from white-oak saplings. "You shave off the bark and splint it at the top," Aiyana explains. "Then you weave the splints in and out. That gives it enough flexibility to move but makes it stronger so the splints don't come off. On the bottom you carve a handle, sometimes with a design." In the past, scrubs were in great demand among non–Native businesses and homes in eastern Long Island, and Aiyana's uncle used to support himself making and selling them.

And, of course, there is dancing at powwows. "I've been dancing since I could walk," Aiyana says. "Ever since I was a baby, my mom would take me to powwows and I'd always dance. It's really important to me! I get a good feeling when I'm dancing. It makes me happy and proud. It's one of my favorite things to do!"

Most of the children on the reservation dance as well but, unlike Aiyana, they tend to stop when they enter adolescence. "When they get to be around pre-teen, or teenagers, a lot of kids don't think it's cool anymore," Aiyana explains. "But after a few years, a lot of times they go back," she adds.

Within the past ten years, a sweat lodge, a structure used in purification ceremonies, has been built at Aiyana's home. Although other families previously had lodges at their homes, Aiyana's family is currently the keeper of the lodge for the community.

The Shinnecock have also received help from members of other nations in reviving their Native American traditions. "A Dakota friend shared his traditions with us—to use, to pray for our ways and our language to return to us," Aiyana says.

"It's brought our people a lot closer together! We have a bad problem with alcohol and drug abuse, and some people have been rehabilitated through using the sweat lodge and praying and getting closer to the Creator.

"Not everybody participates in it," she adds. "Because there's a large percentage who are churchgoers, who are still Presbyterians." For Aiyana, however, Native ceremonies are more meaningful than Christian ones. "When I was little, I used to go to Sunday school. But I never really felt a connection the way that I do with a sweat lodge and things that are closer to nature, more traditional to us."

Although she's leaving next year for college, Aiyana definitely plans to return to the reservation when she finishes her education. "It's like your identity," she explains. "Because you know that this is where you're from, these are your people. And if you went away, you know you can always come back and know that it will still be here. Other places you have to look all over for someone to connect with, but you know it's always here."

There are other reasons as well. "I feel I've been helped by my people, by everyone," Aiyana says. "So, I want to give that back. I want to come back here and help the kids and the community."

She's thought of a number of ways she could do that. "I always pictured myself being a marine biologist, coming back here and working on the shellfish hatchery and getting that together. But I've also been getting really interested in environmental-type things and natural resources."

This past year, however, her plans have begun to shift. "I'm not sure exactly what I want to pursue. I'm not sure if I want to be a teacher or a counselor, but I do think that I want to be in some type of education."

Aiyana feels it's important to include a Native American perspective in the material taught in schools, particularly when the information concerns Native people. The origins of American Indians are a case in point. "I'd emphasize the fact that we were the original people, you know. Because a lot of times, when they talk about us—you know, the whole concept of the Bering Strait* —they say, 'The Indians came from Asia, or whatever, and we wiped them out.'

"They say that life—humans—supposedly started in Africa. But why can't it have been that life started *there*, life started *here*? Why in only one place? It seems like they're always trying to prove that we came from *there*. Instead of just accepting that we were *here*."

Particularly dangerous from Aiyana's point of view is the use of the Bering Strait idea to justify the taking of Indian lands. As she sees it, American history is generally presented as a series of waves of immigration, with each new immigrant group taking control from the one before. By making Native Americans just the first of these waves, instead of the original people, the loss of their land is portrayed as part of the natural progression of things, rather than as the theft and betrayal that it was.

Recently, Aiyana took part in a television show about indigenous peoples. "I think it was pretty good,"

---

*The generally accepted explanation of the origins of Native Americans is that they migrated to the Western Hemisphere from Asia during the Ice Age, when a land bridge existed across what is now the Bering Strait.

she says. "I hope that tape will go into the schools, because I want to be able to educate people on issues that not only Native Americans face, but that people all over the world also face, that often get covered up. Because in our school and schools all around, there's a lot of racial prejudice. We need to be educated about each other's cultures, as well as our own."

One of the things Aiyana especially wants others to understand is that Native Americans are not some defeated group that exists only in the pages of history. "We're still here now," she says emphatically. "We've always been here, we're here now, and we'll continue to be here! A lot of people think that we died, that there aren't any Indians. Well, we're still here and we still do the things that we've done for hundreds, thousands of years."

◆◆◆◆◆◆◆◆◆◆◆◆◆◆◆◆◆◆◆◆◆◆◆◆◆◆◆◆◆◆◆◆◆◆

3
ANISHNABE
(OJIBWAY/CHIPPEWA)

Although the Anishnabe (a word meaning "The People") are one of the largest North American tribes, few non-Native people know them by this, their own name for themselves. Instead, they are referred to in history books and in general terminology as the Ojibway or the Chippewa, names given to them by French and English explorers. Today, the Anishnabe also use these names in everyday conversation. Although some call themselves Chippewa, others, like Kristy, Fawn, and Ginew, prefer Ojibway.* It's important to remember, however, that all three terms refer to the same people.

The Anishnabe originally made their home along the shores of Lake Superior in what is now Canada, Michigan, Wisconsin, and Minnesota. A nomadic people, they lived in wigwams made of saplings and birch bark.

Known for their prowess as hunters, the Anishnabe pursued deer and other game in the forests and, in the summer, fished for sturgeon and whitefish. They supplemented their diet of meat and fish with wild plants and collected sap to make maple syrup in the spring.

The birch tree has always had a special importance in the lives of the Anishnabe. Skilled craftspeople, they fashioned birch bark into containers, cooking vessels, and lightweight canoes that served as the major form of transportation in the Great Lakes region.

Although they lived in areas far from the initial sites

---

*Because Ginew also has Cree ancestry, he is actually an Ojibway/Cree.

of European settlement, the Anishnabe were in contact with European fur traders—particularly French trappers—since the first appearance of Europeans in North America. Because the trappers were few in number and far from their own people, they were quick to establish good relations with Native people, often marrying among them. As a result, many Anishnabe, like Kristy, have some French Canadian ancestry.

Today there are about 15,000 Anishnabe living on reservations in various states of the north-central United States. Many more live in Canada or outside of reservations in this country.

Kristy and her cousin, Fawn, are from the Bay Mills Indian Reservation in Michigan. With 1,085 members, it is one of the smaller Anishnabe communities. The reservation consists of two parts—1,580 acres on the shore of Whitefish Bay near Sault Sainte Marie, where most people live, and another 600 acres on Sugar Island between Michigan and Canada.

Ginew is from the Roseau River Indian Reservation in southern Canada and the Lac Courte Oreilles Indian Reservation in Wisconsin. He is currently living on the Shinnecock Reservation in New York.

BAY MILLS INDIAN RESERVATION
BRIMLEY, MICHIGAN
AND
ROSEAU RIVER INDIAN RESERVATION
MANITOBA, CANADA

We have to be proud of who we are. And never be convinced by other people that our race is bad or that we're stupid. Because it's not that way! I did pretty good in school last year. I was an honor roll student.

—Kristy

We have to keep our heads up and tell ourselves we can do it, no matter how bad people treat us. If we're not going to get help with our education, then we have to do it on our own.

—Fawn

In winter, the shoreline of Whitefish Bay freezes over and a thick blanket of snow covers the Bay Mills Indian Reservation. Like the rest of the snowbound Upper Peninsula of Michigan, it is beautiful but very cold. With the coming of warm weather, however, the area draws thousands of vacationers eager to enjoy hiking in the

Kristy LeBlanc, age 13

forests and fishing, boating, and swimming in Lake Superior.

Although the Ojibway have lived in this area for many hundreds of years, it took Kristy a while to appreciate both the place and her culture. "When I was younger, I didn't really know anything about being Native American," she recalls. "I knew I was Anishnabe, but I didn't go to powwows. I didn't really care for any of that, because I wasn't exposed to it."

In fact, Kristy's mind was far from Bay Mills. "I wanted to be an actress or something, and go to New York, or Florida, or Hawaii, or Hollywood . . . something like that. And live there for the rest of my life and be happy and glamorous!

"And then I heard about earthquakes," she adds, laughing. "And hurricanes, and people robbing each other and stabbing each other, and things. And I thought, 'I like it better here, because it's safer.' I started going to powwows, and I started to appreciate that I was Native American and I started to like it here."

Although Kristy has lived in Bay Mills all her life, her cousin, Fawn, didn't move to the reservation until she was five or six. Fawn spent her early childhood in Detroit, where her mother was raised. But then her parents decided to move to Bay Mills, her father's hometown and the place where his relatives live. Fawn has been there ever since.

Even though Fawn spent her early childhood off the reservation, in some ways she has had more exposure to Ojibway culture than has Kristy. "When I lived in Detroit, I traveled to a lot of powwows. So, I was really exposed to it . . . and I still am!"

These days, both Fawn and Kristy are big fans of powwows. As Fawn explains, these gatherings are more than just an occasion to have fun. "It's a time when Native Americans get together and send our prayers up to the Creator," she says.

Although there is a large spiritual component to powwows, the social aspect is very important too. "We just have a good time with people like ourselves . . . where we're not the minority—the white people who come are—and where we [Native Americans] can be all as one."

Both girls did traditional dancing when they were younger, but not now. "In fifth grade, Fawn and I were in the same class. A teacher came in once a week, and we got to dance," Kristy recalls. "Well, Fawn was kind of self-conscious so it was mostly me and Nadine—we'd get up there and dance. Not to be conceited, but we were pretty good!

"But in sixth grade, the teacher didn't come anymore and I didn't go to a lot of powwows. I didn't dance 'cause I didn't have the music, and I need the music to get the beat and everything," Kristy continues.

Unfortunately, by the time she started going to powwows, Kristy had forgotten the dances. "I don't remember a lot of those dances anymore," she says sadly. "It kind of bums me out, because I like to dance. It was a lot of fun!"

Still, she and Fawn enjoy just watching. "Some people don't dance," Fawn says. "They sit out there and watch the people that do, and it's really fun! I go to powwows a lot and I have a lot of fun watching."

"The powwows aren't just for Native Americans," Kristy adds. "They're open to all people. They sell really cool Indian jewelry and other things there."

Fawn is one of the people who make Indian jewelry, some of which she sells. "She makes beaded earrings and stuff like that," Kristy says. "And kids at school all ask her, 'Where did you get those? Those are really cool! I bet they were expensive!'"

"I haven't sold any bracelets, but I make them for myself," Fawn says. "I made an NMU [Northern Michigan University] barrette for my sister—that's her

Fawn Cameron, age 13

college. My mom made Bay barrettes—we're Brimley Bays at school—for me and my sisters. All my teachers asked, 'Where did you get those? They're so pretty!'"

Kids from Bay Mills attend the public school in Brimley, a small, primarily white, town nearby. Fawn and Kristy have friends from there as well as from the reservation. "Let me put it this way," Kristy says. "Fawn's my best, best, best friend. Courtney Harwood, who has no Native American blood at all—or maybe a fingernail-like pinch of Indian blood in her—she's my best, best friend. And then I have best friends."

Despite these friendships, the relationship between the Ojibway and whites is not always as good as it could be. Although white teachers and students admire Fawn's beadwork, at the same time they sometimes put down Indians and Indian culture.

"Just this past week, we had Indian studies in school," Fawn says. "We had a pipe ceremony and the drummers came in and drummed for us and we had speakers. It was real nice, you know. *I* really appreciated it.

"They sing loud and it's high pitched and stuff," Kristy adds. "But it makes you feel better! And for us, it makes us *proud* to be Indian."

"But people in the class were saying, 'Why do we have to do this? This is stupid!' One girl asked the drummers, 'Don't you ever get a headache from this when you drum?'"

Not surprisingly, the girl's question angered Kristy. "My mouth dropped down to my feet!" Kristy recalls. "I just looked at her. I wanted to go up to her and smack her, but I'm not the kind of person who goes up to people and tells them what I really want to say to them."

Fawn is more outspoken. "I do!" she exclaims. "If I feel something about that person, I will tell them. There is no doubt in my mind! Especially when it comes to *racism*, I will tell them exactly how I feel!"

Unfortunately, some of the teachers seem prejudiced

as well, although they show it in more subtle ways. "There's a teacher at the school," Fawn explains, "who was giving all the people from Bay Mills E's [a failing grade] and telling them that they didn't do it properly, when people from Brimley were doing the exact same thing."

"It *hurts*!" Kristy adds. "One of my friends does something good in school and I have the same answer or I say the same thing, yet I get it wrong. Or if we've got our hands up in class for them to help, they go over and talk to other people who don't even have their hands raised."

The school is supposed to offer classes in the Ojibway language, but to the girls' disappointment, that hasn't happened yet. "They're getting school funding for Native American classes, but they don't have them," Fawn says with disgust. "They're just wasting our money!"

People from Bay Mills deal with these situations in different ways. Recently, a teacher treated Fawn's older sister badly and her family boycotted the school in protest. When other families indicated they were going to show their support by walking out as well, the superintendent stepped in. The students returned to school and things have improved somewhat, but the problem hasn't been completely resolved.

Kristy and Fawn handle most incidents on their own, however. When two boys started making prejudiced remarks, Fawn pointed out to them that they owe their livelihood to Indians. "Their dad's a commmercial fisherman, and he gets all his money from Indians," Kristy explains. "I didn't want to say anything because I didn't want to get anything started, but Fawn says, 'If it wasn't for Indians, you guys would be broke!'"

Not only is Bay Mills a small community, but most people are related to each other in some way, so the death of one person is felt in many families. In addtion, while Kristy and Fawn are close to both of their parents, they feel a special connection to other older relatives as well. The past year has been particularly difficult for them. "There have been a lot of deaths around here," Kristy says. "My aunt died, three of my cousins, my uncle . . ."

While the girls grieve for relatives they loved, the reservation as a whole feels the loss of respected older people who form the backbone of Native American communities. As Fawn laments, "We're losing our elders."

The attitude toward older people is one thing that Fawn and Kristy think separates Native American kids from other teenagers. "We have a lot of respect for all our elders," Kristy says. "When other people in the suburbs or city see an elder drop something—the people walk by and they don't even bother to help them."

"We go out of our way to help," Fawn says. "Like Hank—elderly people around here need help with their yard or something—he'll be happy to help them, and so will his crew."

One of the good things about living on the reservation is that, in general, it's a safe and secure place to be. People all know each other and care more about each other than in many other communities. Like everywhere else, however, Bay Mills has some people who cause trouble.

"You've got to watch out for the people with an alcohol problem," Fawn says. "We know who everybody is, what kind of problems they have."

Some of these individuals are people Fawn and Kristy know very well. "Alcohol is a problem everywhere [in the country], but unfortunately you have to admit there's a lot of it here," Kristy comments. "A lot of my family—I have a very *big* family—have problems with drinking, and they're still in high school, or else they haven't got a job yet.

"People are realizing they don't want to put up with this anymore. Because it gets really hard, with [young people] drinking more, getting into drugs more."

Part of the problem is that there hasn't been much for adolescents to do in Bay Mills. In an effort to provide teenagers with a place to go, the reservation established a teen group, the Soaring Spirits.

"The group's a lot of help," Kristy says. "I have friends around here who are not doing too well at the moment. They have a lot of problems. But coming to group is helping them, because it's showing us how to deal with our problems."

"All of us being together, we're trying to help each other," Fawn adds. "We're trying real hard!"

At thirteen, Fawn and Kristy haven't thought too much about their plans for the future. One thing Fawn's positive about, though, is that she wants to return to Bay Mills after she's finished school. "I love this place!" Fawn says. "I'm going to go to college, come back, and then work in town or something. I want to stay here, or else move to another Indian reservation.

"I'll get a week job and I'll travel on weekends to powwows," she adds. "That's what I want to do!"

Kristy isn't so sure. "I'm still not really sure about college," she says. "I *hate* school nowadays.

"I don't know. I want to be working . . . to have a really good-paying job, one that doesn't involve math," she adds, laughing.

Kristy also wants to see the world. "I'm not going to live around here for the rest of my life! I'm going to experience different places," she exclaims. "I'm not going to buy a house right away. I want to live in an apartment to see where I like it.

"I'm not going to be considering a family," she continues. "'Cause that's a lot of responsibility. I know, because I baby-sit almost every day! I can't say that I'm going to have this tremendous job with a wonderful husband and a kid. . . . I might not even want to get married until I'm forty-five or something."

If Kristy does decide to get married, however, she wants her husband to be a Native American. While marrying another Native person didn't used to matter so much to her, in the past year she's learned a lot more about her culture. As a result, it's become very important to her that her children be brought up traditionally. "If I were to marry a white," she explains, "things wouldn't be the same."

As both girls are aware, Indian heritage tends to get lost with intermarriage. "I don't want our culture to be just a little bit Indian and then a lot of white," Kristy continues. "When I'm sixty-five, I still want there to be full-blooded Indians."

Fawn feels the same way. "I'd *love* to marry a Native person! If I get married, it will be to a Native person! I mean, there's these great guys from Brimley, and I think they're *real fine*," she says, laughing. "But I tell my friends, 'I always want to marry an Indian.' That way, my kids can be raised with Indian culture."

When they think about the relationship between Native Americans and other people, there are some definite changes that Fawn and Kristy would like to see.

"I don't like the way people treat Native Americans," Fawn says. "Like on TV, they don't show us as we are. They show us as barbarians who go around killing the whites. As people who are just doing bad things. They always show the white people as good guys. Like cowboys and Indians—the Indians were always the barbarians, and the cowboys had to go kill them."

"They'll pick these actors, like white people who have dyed hair with their bangs cut, and wearing headdresses," Kristy says with disgust.

"I can't even watch TV like that!" Fawn exclaims. "I just change the channel and won't even look at it. I roll my eyes and keep going!"

"They really didn't know how our culture was," Kristy adds. "There are movies that have a tipi and a totem pole together. That doesn't make any sense, because the totem poles were up toward Canada and the tipis were in the plains with the buffalo. We had the wigwam, and down below us in Ohio and Kentucky were the long houses, and then over in New Mexico were [the homes] they dug out of rock."

"It makes me angry!" Fawn says. "Obviously, they don't want to do the research on the Indians that they should be doing if they're going to put stuff about us on TV. That *hurts*! They don't realize what our feelings are. They just do it to make money."

The movies are painful not only because they misrepresent Indian people but also because they are a reminder of the abuses Native Americans have suffered. "It's really sad when white people put us down like that," Kristy continues. "Because they came over here and they automatically claimed that this land was theirs. But when they found the Indians . . ."

"They put them on reservations," Fawn interjects. "To get them out of their way."

"I'm not ashamed of living where I am, but still, it's sad the way they treated us. What they put our ancestors through is really sad," Kristy says.

Thus, it's a pleasant surprise when a movie comes along that presents Native people accurately. "There are only two movies that I have ever seen that I actually enjoyed with Native American people in them," Kristy continues. "*Thunderheart*, that was an awesome movie! And then there was another one, *Dances with Wolves*.

"I feel good about them because they show how we really lived, how our ancestors really lived. And they respect that and they tell it that way," she says. "It's a story that *could* have happened and probably *did* in some way happen with our ancestors."

In addition to wishing their history and culture were accurately portrayed, Fawn and Kristy want people to understand what Native Americans are like today.

"We're no different from other people except for our culture, and the way that our ancestors lived and our dark skins," Kristy says. "We're into heavy metal, pop, rap, and all this other kind of stuff. People think that because once all of our tribespeople had hair down to here and wore headbands and moccasins that we're different from everybody else. But it's not like that anymore. We're definitely normal people!" she adds.

"It's kind of funny when you're watching a movie on Indian culture and people who aren't Native Americans sit there watching and go, 'Wow! They really did *that*?!'

"If Indians catch a deer and skin it, they say, 'Oh yuck! They did that to those animals, those poor animals?' It's funny watching them when they do that, because their ancestors did the same thing."

"We like the same kind of music and stuff. We like to wear all the same kinds of clothes as they do," Fawn says. "They'll ask, 'What kind of clothes do you-all wear?' Well, take a look! Everyone likes designer clothes. Of course, they do!"

"I just wish they could see us as we are," Fawn concludes." As normal people. As *humans*!"

Ginew spent his early childhood on the Ojibway reservations of Roseau River in Manitoba and Lac Courte Oreilles in Wisconsin. But when his mother married Aiyana's uncle, the family moved to the Shinnecock Reservation. "It was the summer after second grade," Ginew recalls. "I'm in eighth grade now, so it was about six years ago."

Ginew Benton, age 13

Initially, the transition was somewhat difficult. Complicating things was the fact that some Shinnecock kids weren't too happy with the idea of a non-Shinnecock—even if he was a Indian—living on the reservation. "Not all the kids were so nice, you know," his stepfather says. "Some of the kids resented him. It made it hard for him because some people considered him an outsider."

This was very different from the atmosphere on his own reservation in Canada, or on his father's reservation in Wisconsin, where he was unconditionally accepted. As is true of all Native Americans, no matter where they go or how long they are gone, their place among the people on their home reservation is secure.

"I have a lot of people—there's over a hundred people on my other reservation, at home, who are related to me," Ginew says. Relatives or not, however, "they treat me like I'm a brother."

Although Ginew has been away for the past six years, he is always on the minds of those at home and people still recognize his voice when he calls on the phone. Knowing that he has a place where he belongs, that he can always return to and be welcomed, made it easier to cope with the initial problems he had on the Shinnecock Reservation.

Recently, things have improved for Ginew and there are many things he likes about living with the Shinnecock now, including the friends he has made. And, unlike some teenagers who find reservation life boring, Ginew can always think of interesting things to do. "Yesterday, we went clamming," he says, even though it was one of the coldest days in the year. "We bundled up, really bundled up," Ginew continues. "And we went out on the water—it was frozen over and it was low tide."

January may seem a strange time of year to dig for clams, but it's actually easier to spot their breathing holes when it's cold. "They're just sleeping," explains Ginew. "You have to look for spots the ice hasn't gotten to yet, where it's melted away in pieces. You can see that there's little holes in the rocks that go down to the clams. You make a hole, dig, find the clam, and just put it in a bucket. We got thirteen clams," he adds.

He and his friends also do other things that are based in their Native American culture. "We make wickiups—it's an upside-down bowl-shaped house made of sticks and bark and sometimes straw," he says. "And we go hunting sometimes with Charlie [his stepfather]— with a bow and arrow." Killing things is never done as a sport, however. The rule is, if you hunt it, you have to eat it.

At one time, the Shinnecock people had land all over the east end of Long Island. Now, only a small piece remains. Yet, the neighboring community continues to try to take even that. "That's the true meaning of a reservation," Ginew says. "It's land that was thought to be worthless and was given to Native Americans. That's how it was here. They thought this land was worthless a long time ago. Now they want it because it got really valuable. It has a lot of space and woods. And outside the Southampton area, there's no space. It's nothing but houses and cars."

He has trouble understanding how people can be so arrogant. "I just say, 'How would you feel if I wanted to take your land for a driveway or something?' It seems like people just can't get enough of what they have," he adds. "It's conceited, greedy!"

Although the Shinnecock have no intention of giving up any of their land, outsiders are encroaching in other, more subtle ways. "You can see white people driving up and down the roads," Ginew explains. "Even though the signs say, 'Private property. Keep out! Indian Reservation.'" Even worse, when the town dump began charging fees, some local residents started to throw their garbage onto more isolated parts of the reservation, where they were unlikely to get caught.

"It makes me feel like I don't like them!" he adds angrily. "It's just the same thing as driving through a forest where signs everywhere say, 'No smoking.' And a guy smokes, throws his cigarette out, and burns down the whole forest."

Since there is no school on the reservation, Shinnecock students attend public schools in Southampton. Like many Native American young people, Ginew often finds himself caught between the expectations and goals of a white school system and the traditional values he was raised with.

"The value system in white schools is competitive, to compete with the other students and to try to be better than everyone else," his mother explains. "The value system of Native Americans is that everyone helps everyone else do better. If someone's not doing well, it's your responsibility to help them out."

Being assertive, such as standing up and speaking in class or trying to get the teacher to call on you, is not a traditional value either. "The traditional value is the opposite—to be respectful and to let your elders and others speak before you," she says.

Ginew consistently gets A's and B's. But because he's so quiet, it doesn't always register with his teachers how well he's doing. Although they're aware he's a good student in their classes, it frequently doesn't occur to them that he might be getting good grades in all his other classes as well. As a result, in the fourth grade, they overlooked him in giving out the Presidential Academic Fitness Award. "I would have been the only Native American in that grade to get the Presidential Award," Ginew says with regret.

When the school's error was pointed out, Ginew eventually got the Presidential Award. But it was too late to receive it at the public ceremony or to get his name in the paper with the others, and that hurt. "While class was going they said over the loud speaker, 'Sorry for this interruption, but we overlooked somebody. Ginew Benton received the award. Thank you.' But that's not the same as getting it in front of everybody," he adds.

Ironically, he did get the art award—mainly because he's talented but also because his teachers expect him, as an Indian, to be creative, so they notice his artistic abilities.

While Ginew may be shy in the white world, in his own community he's a very different person. The young man who hates standing up in front of his class has absolutely no problem getting up in front of thousands of people and competing as a Native American dancer. "It's just that I like it and I'm used to it," he says.

Ginew is a champion grass dancer (a traditional dance), although he dances for the love of it, not to win prizes. His dancing also has a special, spiritual quality that has brought him acknowledgment from Native Americans. "One of the things that's said about him in his dancing is that he has spirit," his mother explains. "There's a spirit that not all people have when they dance. It's as if someone who has gone on [an ancestor] is dancing with him." As far as Ginew is concerned, dancing is a major part of his life. "I don't think I'll ever quit!" he says emphatically.

In addition to dancing, drumming, and singing at powwows, Ginew participates in other ceremonies. The most important of these was his Coming of Age Ceremony, held last summer. This ceremony marks the time when teenagers formally accept the responsibility for establishing their own connections with the Creator and developing their own spirituality. A year earlier, when he was twelve, Ginew began to feel that he was ready to start preparing for the ceremony.

"It takes a year to get ready for it," Ginew explains. The young person must not only prepare mentally and spiritually, but must also save money to pay for the feast and the gifts that are a part of the occasion. Ginew was able to accumulate $1,200 in prize winnings from the dance competitions he had entered at various powwows. "I also made a lot of things for my 'give away,'" he continues. "I made fifteen sand paintings and framed them for gifts."

The Shinnecock allowed him to hold the ceremony in a special area of the reservation, and he invited them to the feast. Relatives from his home reservation and his father's reservation also came for the occasion.

From among the older men he respected, Ginew picked sponsors to help guide him through the ceremony. These men will also be people he can turn to for the rest of his life, for guidance and advice, so choosing his sponsors was a serious decision.

"First, we made a lodge for the feast out of saplings and branches,"* Ginew explains. "Then we [he and his sponsors] went away from everyone else to another part of the woods." There they purified themselves in a special sweat lodge and Ginew fasted for two days.

The experiences and visions Ginew had while fasting were the most important part of the ceremony, for it is through them that a young person connects to the Creator and learns lifelong spiritual lessons. "While I was fasting," Ginew continues, "a deer and her fawn stayed by me. They weren't afraid of me at all! A butterfly visited me too and an old woman [a vision, not a physical woman] came and sang for me. Oh, and a cricket sang me to sleep."

Afterward, Ginew and his sponsors joined his guests at the feast. At this time, the young person shares the events of the past two days with the others, explaining what they meant. For everyone at the feast, this was a very powerful experience. "Even little kids sat still for hours," Ginew says. "Because they could tell it was something different, something really important."

It was also a particularly moving experience for some of the Shinnecock raised with a conventional Christian background. Although their church has always been an important spiritual force in their lives, many

---

*You can see part of the lodge in the photo on page 65.

said they had never felt as close to God as they did on that day.

Much of tradition consists of formal ceremonies or things that a young person is taught, but a lot is learned simply by being around elders and talking to them. One of Ginew's elders is his great-uncle, who was also one of his sponsors.

"He's an old, down-to-earth man," says Ginew. "He has long hair. He's really traditional. When he came out here, he wanted to do everything. We went up to Montauk, to the point. And he told me to get a sample of the water and of the sand, and put it in a jar." When his uncle has ceremonies back in Saskatchewan, Canada, the sand and the water will help to bring Ginew's family closer to him.

His uncle likes talking about the trees and the water, and Ginew enjoys these conversations too. He thinks this pleases the older man. "Because it shows how a real Indian should act. How he should talk about everything, describe them, and take them for what they are," Ginew says. "I think that he likes that I like him talking about it because he knows that I've been brought up right by my mom and my dad. And that I was brought up the old way, and taught to like people for what they are."

Ginew is proud of who he is, and he wishes everyone—particularly Native American kids—would like who they are. "I just want to say out loud, 'Wake up and look in the mirror. See who you are! You're already somebody special!'"

4
QUINAULT

The Northwest Coastal Indians, of whom the Quinault are a part, occupy the narrow rainy coast from the bend in Alaska to the mouth of the Columbia River. Prior to the coming of Europeans, they made their living entirely from the ocean and coastal rivers. Expert canoe builders and sailors, they hunted whales, sea lions, fur seals, and sea otters on the open sea and fished along the rivers for salmon.

The Quinault have always lived on the coast of Washington around the Quinault River. Even before contact with Europeans, they were a small nation, probably numbering no more than 1,200 people. Since it was not always possible to find marriage partners in a group of that size, the Quinault often took spouses from neighboring coastal groups. These marriages helped to cement trading relationships, provided relatives to stay with when traveling, and secured allies in war.

Europeans and Quinaults first encountered each other in the summer of 1775 when Spanish ships anchored near the Quinault River. Although there were occasional skirmishes between whites and Indians of the northwest coast, conflict between the two groups never led to war. But the arrival of whites spelled disaster just the same, for the diseases that accompanied them virtually wiped out the coastal tribes.

Beginning in 1779, epidemic after epidemic of smallpox, influenza, and fever struck the coast, decimating the Indian population. By 1885, only 100 Quinault remained. Even so, they were more fortunate than some tribes to the south, which were completely annihilated.

Today, more than 2,000 people are enrolled in the Quinault Indian Nation. However, modern Quinaults now include people from seven previously separate nations. Thus, while they all consider themselves Quinaults, many have Queets, Hoh, Quileute, Chinook, Chehalis, Cowlitz, or other Indian ancestry.

The 200,000 acres comprising the Quinault Reservation are made up of land originally belonging to two separate nations, the Quinault and the Quileute. In addition to those living on the reservation who identify themselves as Quinaults, there are many descendants of the original Chinook, Chehalis, Hoh, and Quileute tribes who have inherited allotments on the Quinault Reservation but who are not members of the Quinault Indian Nation.

The ancestry of Stanley and his sister, Lolita, reflects the intermarriages that have historically taken place among Native American nations on the coast of Washington. Although they are primarily of Quinault descent, their great-grandmother was a full-blooded Quileute, and their great-great-grandfather was a Yakima Indian. Stanley and Lolita also have many relatives on the Makah Indian Reservation at Neah Bay and among the Yurok in California.

QUINAULT INDIAN RESERVATION
TAHOLAH, WASHINGTON

I have a cousin the same age as I am—we grew up together. We'd go to my grandmother's every day and do chores for her. Then she'd sit us down and tell us a lot of stories and myths and legends. Once in a while, she'd sing us Indian songs.

—Stanley

Some kids, they really don't know their heritage and what it was like a long time ago. I know some of my heritage from being around my great-grandmother. She told me and my cousins stories, legends, and about our culture.

—Lolita

From Lake Quinault in the Olympic Mountains, the Quinault River flows through dense, moss-laden coniferous forests and over thousands of waterfalls as it journeys to the Pacific coast. At the mouth of the river, where it joins the ocean, lies Taholah, the primary town on the Quinault Reservation and the home of Stanley and Lolita.

"We have a nice river here," Stanley says. "Up and

down the river, there's eagles flying around, there's deer and bear on the sides of the river—not as much now as, say, ten years ago, even five years ago, because there's so much logging around here. But there's good meat out there.

"The beach is good to walk up and down. I do it now, just up and down the beach. It calms me down—or livens me up, depends," he adds, smiling.

Stanley started drawing pictures of these things when he was a small child. "One Christmas, my dad gave me a little drafting board. Every little piece of paper that had something good on it, I'd trace it down," he remembers.

"I usually draw animals, trees, water, the ocean, river—nature. That's the Northwest Coastal style. Ever since the seventh grade, I started getting into Northwest Coastal style."

Stanley has been fortunate to have as a friend an older Quinault artist, Guy Capoeman, who encourages and guides him. "He's taught me a lot," Stanley says. "I don't like saying it . . . but I'm fairly good. But a lot of my drawing was just for looks, you know, because it looked good. Since I ran into Guy a couple of years ago, he started telling me, 'You should put some kind of meaning into your art. Something that tells a story, gives feelings.' So, I've been trying that."

Although he's still in high school, Stanley already has a beginning career. "I sell a lot of my artwork," he says. "I'm always busy. I've done ten things already this half of the school year. I've still got quite a big order."

Eventually, Stanley would like to go to college in Santa Fe, New Mexico. "A teacher came in from Santa Fe, and he told me that would be the best school to go to for Indian art. A lot of other people are saying that that's the art capital for Native Americans," Stanley says. He's now in the process of getting a portfolio together so he can apply.

Fortunately for Stanley, there's financial support for him to do what he wants. "There's no kids around here who can't go to college or get whatever they want in life, 'cause the tribe's right here to support us," he explains. "They encourage us to go off to school. They'd do practically anything to see to that."

Afterward, Stanley plans to come back to Taholah, although maybe not right away. "Yeah, I'll come back. I've lived here all my life, and it's my life," he says. "I'm not sure exactly what I'm going to do after school. I may come straight back, I may stay around Santa Fe and show my art, 'cause it is the art capital."

Lolita's life revolves around her two-year-old son, James. "He's very important to me," she says. "I love him with all my heart! James is my highlight—if I didn't have him, I don't know what I would do!"

Lolita considers herself lucky because both her friends and her family stood by her when she was pregnant. "Most teenage girls, when they become pregnant, their friends and family get upset and tell them, 'You got pregnant by yourself, so you can take care of the baby by yourself.' But I'm one of the lucky ones, because my parents are really helpful. They love me a lot and they love James a lot. James brings light into our lives, especially to my grandmother, Helene."

Stanley clearly enjoys his nephew. "He's a real character! I'm amazed. He's got opinions in his own way. He's got his own little personality. We have a blast together!"

James was almost born on Stanley's birthday, something he would have loved. "It was really cool—well, almost cool," he says. "It would have been awesome if he'd been born on my day. She went into the hospital on my birthday, but it was false labor."

As much as Lolita loves James and as happy as she is to have him, it's been difficult to be a teenage single mother. "It's hard," Lolita admits. "My grandmother watches James while I go to school. If she feels sick, my father or my aunt watches him for me. But if they can't, I have to stay home from school."

James's father is a Yurok Indian who was living with his mother right outside the Quinault Reservation. "I met James's dad, and we went out for about a year and a half, two years," Lolita says. "I broke up with him when I was seven months pregnant because he had started to drink a lot."

"He lives in California with his dad now," Lolita continues. "We tried getting back together but it didn't work out between us. He stopped drinking and all, but we just didn't get along like we used to, so we said let's just be friends."

Lolita knows he loves James, and she wants him to be a part of her son's life. "I know that later James will ask where his dad is, what he's like, and when can he meet him. One of the reasons why he moved back down to California is to get his life back together. He's finishing school—he's going to junior college right now—and he has a part-time job," she says.

"When he was here, he dropped out of school. It was his senior year, and he dropped out. It was kind of hard for me to accept that he dropped out and to accept that he started to drink. It was real hard, because we had fun together," she adds.

Finding someone else has been complicated because she has a child, but recently she met someone she really likes and feels comfortable with. "It was kind of hard to find someone, because some guys don't like seeing someone who has a child," she explains. "But I'm seeing someone now and he has a kid of his own and I have my child. We get along great! And he really likes James. He cares about all three of us a lot!"

Although Lolita has been able to succeed as a young mother, she advises other young women to wait to have children until they're older. "I'm in a teen panel—

Lolita Black, age 18, Stanley Black, age 19

TAPPP—it stands for Teenage and Pregnancy, Parenting, Prevention Program. We go around to different schools and we do workshops. The kids ask us questions and we answer them. We try to get teenagers to use protection so they won't get pregnant, and to wait to have their family until they have an education."

Until a few years ago, students from the reservation attended a regular public high school in Moclips, a town ten miles away. "There was a little bit of prejudice, but there wasn't that much," Stanley says, describing his experience there. "We were more athletic, so we ruled sports there. See, when we were in seventh and eighth grades, we used to play them in basketball, football, and baseball. Those two years, we dominated pretty much everything. So, when we started going to high school with them, they knew us. It was all right being together, they weren't that bad."

Lolita was very comfortable there. "I went there for two years," she says. "It was fun while it lasted! I met a lot of other people, different friends. I had a lot of fun there."

But when a new school was built farther south, everyone was transferred. "It took us an hour to get there," Stanley recalls. "We had to catch two buses, and we had to wake up early—too early! I used to have to get up at five-thirty, six-thirty, just to catch the bus."

Shortly thereafter, the high school at Taholah was completed, and Quinault students now go to school on the reservation. Thus, with the exception of a few non-Native kids who live in the district, the students at Taholah are all Indians.

The new school has its pluses and minuses. The most obvious advantage is that it's close to home. "I really like it, 'cause now we can sleep till seven-thirty," Stanley says. "It's a lot better here," he adds, "But the education level there was higher. I think they could stress education more here."

Lolita feels differently. If the public school hadn't been moved so far away, she would have preferred going there, primarily because the students were better disciplined. "In this school, there's kids that don't go to class, they roam the hall, they go into different classes and when the teachers tell them to go to their own class, they mouth off at the teacher," she says.

With only forty-five to fifty students, Taholah High School is also much smaller than the public high school. "There's about fifteen girls in our school, and about thirty, thirty-five guys," Lolita says.

While that ratio might seem good to other girls, it's not quite the same if the majority of the boys are your relatives. "Most of us here in Taholah are related to almost everybody else," Lolita continues. "I'm probably related to fifty percent of this whole school. There were quite a few guys that I liked, but they turned out to be my cousins."

As in many high schools, sports are a major activity for girls as well as boys. Lolita hopes they can get a girls' softball team together, but it's hard with only fifteen potential players. "I hope we can," she says, "if the girls start to pull their grades up. Because there's quite a few who have real low grades."

Until recently, the Quinault Reservation didn't offer teenagers much in the way of entertainment. "There wasn't anything down here to do—unless you have a car to get out of here," Lolita says. "My aunt Cheryl had a video shop. She'd rent out videotapes, VCRs, and she had video and card games. People would go to her and hang out. Then she had to close it down because of money problems, so we were left without things to do for about a year, year and a half. It was pretty hard, and a lot of teens turned to drugs and alcohol."

Things should improve now, however. "We just got our new youth center, so there's some things to do," she continues. "There's a boxing ring, a weight-lifting room, a game room, and a TV room. Kids can start going to the center, instead of getting into trouble," Lolita says.

Like Stanley, Lolita plans to go to college, but her interest is in computers. "I'm in two computer classes now—keyboard and business computers. I like the way the computer works. In business computers, we're learning DOS right now. I'm learning a lot in this program."

She'd like to come back to Taholah after she graduates from college, but she's not sure. "I would like to come back to my hometown," she says. "But Taholah is changing a lot. The kids used to respect their parents and elders. They never talked back to their parents like the kids do now. There was respect for other people.

"These kids . . . I grew up with them. I think it's drugs that changed them. They think they are the adults and the elders are the children. There's kids that think they are gang members. Last year, they burnt down a preacher's house. It's just getting real awful around here. I don't want James to grow up in this environment. I want the best for my son, not for him to grow up thinking that he's in a gang," she says.

"I want to come back here, because I grew up here. But I'll probably just go to some place where it's decent and see what it's like. . . . Maybe to another reservation."

Stanley feels things have changed too, but in a different way. Many people on the Quinault Reservation support themselves, at least in part, by salmon fishing and logging. But the salmon population has diminished sharply over the past years.

"Fishing has gone down since five years ago," he says. "I remember there being a lot of fish. My dad and I would come home from fishing with a boat full of fish. Nowadays, sometimes you're lucky to get one a week. There's a lot of overfishing out in the ocean—you know, the Japanese, a lot of other people out there. And there's logging on the riverside. All different kinds of factors that come into play affect the fish," he explains.

The Quinault Nation is trying to deal with this problem. "There's a fish hatchery up at Lake Quinault," Stanley continues. "If that wasn't there, it would be much worse. People work up at the hatchery, taking care of fish, and when they're fingerlings, they let them go. They count how many fish they let out in the river and streams every season."

Other Quinault work in both logging and replanting trees that have been cut down. They watch the trees carefully, examining how they grow and timing how long it takes to replace those cut down.

Native Americans bitterly resent stereotypes that label all Indians as being alcoholics or drug addicts. But while it certainly isn't true that most Indians are drunks, people on reservations face the same problems of substance abuse that plague other communities throughout the country.

"I believe every Indian everywhere has tried alcohol or drugs at one time or another," Stanley says. "And some of them get bitten and taken away and they're gone for a long time. Their head's in a bottle. I'm not saying everybody around here's a drunk or anything. I'm saying that at one time or another . . . well, some are lucky, some aren't."

Stanley and Lolita have experienced having someone in their family with a drinking problem. Because of liver damage caused by past drinking, their mother must now live with relatives in another town so that she can be closer to the hospital. And Stanley has had difficulties of his own.

"I was getting in trouble the last five years or so, maybe even longer. You know, getting into all these drugs and stuff," he recalls. After several arrests, the court sent him to a drug treatment program specifically for Native Americans. The program not only helped him deal with drugs; it also motivated him to learn more about his culture.

"It was an Indian treatment center where only Indians go, and they have Indian counselors and staff. There was an Indian there who asked us if we knew any of our language, or culture, or anything. I told him I knew some stuff, but hardly any words. And he'd make us feel small for not knowing," Stanley continues.

Although he had loved listening to the legends and songs his great-grandmother and grandmother told him as a child, he hadn't thought of this knowledge as anything special. "I just took our culture and everything for granted—'it's just culture, nothing important,' you know. I never really kept hold of it because I was thinking they'd be there all my life," he says.

"But after I came back, I just went straight to books, to people that knew about the culture," Stanley continues. "I've been studying Quinault culture since last summer."

Stanley and Lolita are both members of the Quinault Nation Indian Dancers. Stanley has been a part of the group for six or seven years, but he began dancing even earlier as a young child. "Being around my great-grandma Black, she had us moving around, going around in circles. That's always stuck in my head."

When he was older and working in a youth summer program, the leader came into the workplace and asked for people who wanted to dance. Since dancing was more fun than working, most of the kids jumped at the chance. Although many dropped out after the summer program, Stanley has continued to dance.

When Lolita was chosen Miss Quinault Nation, she began dancing too. Now she tries to get others involved as well. "One of the things that I want kids to start doing is Indian dancing, and taking an interest in their culture," she says.

"These are our own dances," she continues. "They're based on legends. The paddle dance, the welcome dance, the whale dance, the elk dance, and the wolf dance.

"I have my older brother, four cousins, and friends in the dance group. So we have fun when we practice," she adds. "Plus, you get to go places and meet new people. You can get in the paper, be on TV. We got on the Discovery Channel! That was really good—except for filming it. It was cold, and we were filming until one-thirty in the morning. But we had fun! We had to wait a couple of months to see ourselves on TV, but it was worth it!"

"We've danced all over Washington State and in parts of Oregon, and we performed at the Goodwill Games," Stanley says. They were also invited to dance in Hawaii. "They had a native basketball tournament— the Hawaiians and the American Indians. They wanted us to entertain afterwards. We were on local TV there," he adds.

Unlike many other Native Americans, the nations of the Pacific Northwest did not historically attend pow-wows. Instead, they held potlatches, huge feasts where hosts distributed costly gifts to guests. Although Quinault may occasionally go to powwows today, they are much more likely to dance at banquets, retirement parties, and other celebrations.

One of these celebrations was for the 100th birthday of Stanley and Lolita's great-grandma Black. "The Quinault Indian Nation Dancers danced for her on her birthday," Stanley says. "I think she liked it. She wasn't able to talk hardly, but I could see from the look in her eye that she was proud of us!"

Lolita intends to continue dancing when she graduates from high school. "And when I go off to college, I'll still dance with our dancers. After I get out of college, I don't know if I'll continue," she says. "But I want to get James started dancing."

In addition to the fun and excitement they've had dancing, Lolita and Stanley enjoy the opportunity to make other people aware of the culture of Quinault Indians. "Every time we dance for someone or we are invited to do a dance, the people like the dances we do for them," Lolita says. "They watch us, and they're really interested."

"I have pride in that [being on TV]—showing off our culture to people," Stanley adds. "I really take pride in all that I do for my tribe!"

5
PUEBLO INDIANS

Around the year A.D. 750, a group of people in New Mexico called the Anasazi, or "Ancient Ones," began to build distinctive homes out of adobe, or mud. Over the years, they developed the technique of placing these structures one on top of the other, with each level set back so that the roof of the lower level served as the front yard of the one above. The results of this innovation were villages of multitiered, multiroom apartment buildings. The largest of these, Pueblo Bonito in Chaco Canyon, had 800 rooms and reached a height of five stories.

Starting about A.D. 1300, the Anasazi left these large villages for reasons that are unclear. They migrated to the south, many settling near the Rio Grande in central New Mexico, and established similar but smaller villages.

The Spanish explorers who first encountered these farming communities in 1540 referred to them as pueblos, the Spanish word for town. The term is now used to refer to the multitiered homes, the people, and the culture of Native Americans who occupy these permanent adobe villages.

Today, there are approximately 35,000 Pueblo Indians from nineteen pueblos in New Mexico and nine in northeastern Arizona. They speak six different languages and, in other parts of the country, would be considered separate tribes. However, because they share so many cultural features and are located so close to each other, they are generally grouped together.

The Pueblo of San Ildefonso, where Shawna lives, is located north of Santa Fe. Established in the 1300s or early 1400s, it is one of five pueblos where Tewa is spoken. With just under 700 people and 26,100 acres, San Ildefonso is one of the smaller pueblos.

Loretta lives in Jemez Pueblo, the only pueblo where Towa is spoken. With 89,000 acres and more than 3,000 people, Jemez is much larger than San Ildefonso. Jemez Pueblo has been at its present site northwest of Albuquerque since 1400.

SAN ILDEFONSO PUEBLO
NEW MEXICO
AND
JEMEZ PUEBLO
NEW MEXICO

It's a good feeling to be noticed, to have people know that we're around, what we're like and everything.
— *Shawna*

We're a proud people. We're proud of our heritage. I think it's important that people know that we are here, we're going to stay here, and we're not going away!
— *Loretta*

The arid mesas, canyons, mountains, and deserts of the Pueblo Indians are very different from the green forests of Bay Mills, Taholah, or Cherokee. New Mexico is different in another way as well. Here, the impact of Native Americans on mainstream culture is visible everywhere. Three groups of people—Indians, Hispanics, and Anglos [non-Hispanic whites]—make up the population of New Mexico. Yet all share the turquoise and silver jewelry, adobe architecture, and the food of the original Native people.

In varying proportions, these three groups can be found in most public schools. Shawna attends high school in Espanola, where the students are primarily Indian and Hispanic. As she reports, "Everyone gets along pretty well."

In fact, because of the competition between pueblos, Shawna doesn't think she'd like going to a school that was strictly for Indians. "Everyone would say their pueblo's better than the other person's," she says.

Loretta went to public high school in Albuquerque, approximately forty-five miles away. Although it's somewhat unusual for students to go this far from home, it's becoming more common.

"More and more are starting to go to Albuquerque," Loretta says. "There's elementaries around here and there's a couple elementaries here in the pueblo. There's a high school up in Canon, up north. The majority [of high school students] go there. But there's also a few that go to Santa Fe Indian School or St. Catherine's Indian School—those are boarding schools."

Because of the difficulty in traveling back and forth every day, Loretta's parents rented an apartment in Albuquerque for her. Although her father stayed with her a lot, there were times when she was completely on her own.

While some parents might be nervous about leaving a teenager alone, Loretta says, "My parents knew that I wasn't going to do anything dumb, like throw parties or stay out all hours. They never really enforced a curfew on me, but I knew when to come home. I'm not stupid, where I'm not going to come home for three days!"

After graduating from high school, Loretta took a semester off from school and her parents gave up the

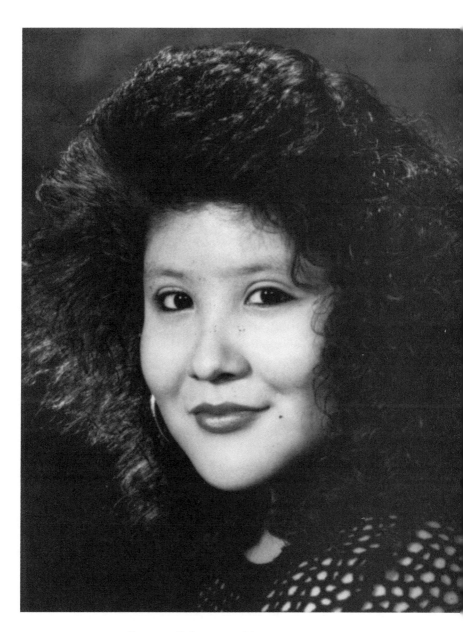

Loretta Cajero, age 18

apartment. But now that she attends community college in Albuquerque, she wishes she had it back!

Her father takes her to Albuquerque now. "He works there as an education specialist," Loretta continues. "I've got to get up at four-thirty every morning so we can leave by six." With this schedule, she has to go to sleep pretty early. "I get to bed by ten, ten-thirty at the latest," she adds.

Despite the traveling, there are good things about this arrangement. "I liked living in Albuquerque, because it was so convenient to school—and to be in the city in general," Loretta recalls. "But on the weekends, I couldn't wait to come home! Because this is home, you know. This is where I grew up, this is where my family is."

Shawna also likes living on the pueblo, although she admits there are some disadvantages. San Ildefonso is a very small place, so everyone always knows what everyone else is doing.

"The good thing about being here is that you know you're safe because everybody knows each other and they'll protect you," she says. "But the thing I hate is that it's such a small pueblo that everybody hears everything and you can't keep anything a secret."

While life in San Ildefonso is very secure, it can get a little boring. "There's nothing to do around here," Shawna comments. "For fun, we have to go out of here, to Santa Fe or something." Most teenagers don't get the opportunity to do that very often, however.

"It gets tiresome going out with your friends," she continues. "You get bored with it." Some kids handle this by branching out to other pueblos. "They'll hang around here with the same people. But then it gets old and they'll go out to different pueblos and start making friends with everybody else. All of a sudden, they'll be all over the place!"

Now that she's almost out of school, Shawna sometimes considers moving, but it would be hard for her to leave San Ildefonso. "I think about moving away," she says. "But then when I think about it, I want to just come back—because I've been here all my life, and I don't know how to live on my own."

If she did decide to go, it would probably be to California. She's been to her godparents' home near Los Angeles and liked the area. "But then it's such a big place and everything," she sighs.

Loretta has traveled to other states as well. She recently visited her sister and brother-in-law in Missouri and was not impressed. "We were there for six weeks back in November," she recalls. "And it rained, and it was cold, and I thought, 'How can you take it?'

"There's these tiny rolling hills, and they called them mountains. I said, 'Those aren't mountains! Those are hills. I'm sorry, but those are not mountains!' And when I got home, I looked to the Sandias and I said, 'See! *Those* are mountains!'"

Pueblo Indians are known worldwide for their artistry, particularly as pottery makers. Galleries throughout New Mexico handle their work, and Pueblo pottery is featured in many museums. Both Shawna and Loretta come from families of successful artists, but neither plans to enter this field herself.

"They're all mainly pottery makers and artists in my family," Shawna says. "My cousin—he draws. My mother and grandmother make pottery. My mother sells around here. And my grandmother—people from all over order from her."

Shawna has different interests, however. "Anything to do with computers!" she replies, when asked what area she'd like to work in. "I'm really good at math and all that. All I want to do is computers!"

Loretta doesn't want to make pottery either. "I'm

more into the business aspect," she says. "I don't like making pottery. It gets boring, and I get dirty, and I don't like it at all!"

With so many artists in her family, there was a lot of pressure on Loretta to become one too. "They thought I'd most likely follow in their footsteps, making pottery. Everybody was always telling me, 'You can make pottery, and you can make money.' And I know I can, but I don't like to. It's not my thing!

"My mom, she finds joy in it, and my brother finds joy in it, my sister-in-law and my sister help them, and they find joy in it, but I *don't*—I don't find the joy in it.

"When we go to art shows, I sell their stuff for them. I negotiate prices," Loretta continues. "That's *my* contribution."

Loretta enjoys the psychological challenge involved in getting a good price from a customer. "One woman wanted to negotiate a price, and my mom let me handle it," she recalls. "The piece was originally priced for twelve hundred dollars, I think. And my mom said, 'Try to go for eight hundred at least.' So, I said, 'How about eight seventy-five?' And she said, 'How about eight hundred?' And I said, 'All right.' So, I got what I wanted and I made her think that she talked me down," she says with a smile.

Not surprisingly, her family has come to appreciate her talents as a businesswoman. "My mom always tells people, 'She's my saleswoman. She sells my stuff for me.'"

Loretta's plan is to continue at a community college for a few years, then transfer to the University of New Mexico. "Right now I'm focusing on Native businesses," she says. "My mom's trying to start this business and I'm trying to get the background that I need to help her in every way that I can. I just have to get myself educated first to know how everything works."

She's already gotten a good foundation from a

course she took in high school. "It helped me to understand the value of our pieces," she says. "And to try not to let anybody railroad us into selling them for less than they're worth. Because it's very hard to work on them. The whole process is so hard and so rigorous," she adds. "And I will not have someone trying to tell me to sell something for thirty-five when I know I could get eighty for it. I don't see it that way!"

In her senior year, Loretta did a project on how to start her own business. "It was a competition in small business ownership and management. I took it to state, and I won first place!" she says proudly. "And then I went to nationals in Orlando, Florida, and I placed in the top twenty in my category."

As far as she could tell, she was the only Indian person at the nationals. "It looked like I was the only Native American there," she continues. "My mom and I were trying to find someone—we can usually spot each other—but we couldn't find anybody."

Thus, while she was very proud and happy to be there, she also wishes there had been a bigger representation of Native people. "A lot of Indian kids aren't focused in that sort of way," Loretta says. "They're just trying to survive day by day. Because there's a lot of prejudice out there still."

Loretta feels a big part of the problem is that Native American teenagers are torn between two cultures. "There's a lack of understanding of them because they're trying to balance two worlds," she explains. "They're trying to keep their Indian culture and they're trying to keep their heritage alive, but yet they've got to balance this with the new modern world—to do English, math, whatever. They have to do both without clashing them, and it's hard! It's real hard!"

Often, young people miss important ceremonies because they have to go to school. "It used to be that they didn't count your religious holidays against you,"

Loretta says. "But the school attendance policy got stricter and stricter and it got to the point that it was an absence no matter what.

"In those situations, your heart is always here, but no matter how much you want to be here for certain things, you do what you've got to do. The same way with people who work."

Conflicting obligations posed by work and school are not the only difficulties Native Americans face in keeping their cultures alive. White exploitation of cultural events presents an equally dangerous threat. "Outsiders come in to witness our ceremonies that used to be sacred," Loretta says. "Then they start trying to market things that they have seen, like maybe photographs, or if one of them is a painter, he paints a picture of what he's seen."

Loretta feels very strongly that this must not be permitted. "That's precisely the reason that at our feast, there's a sign saying, 'Don't tape-record. Don't photograph. Don't sketch.' And there's people around who, if they see you trying to take anything of that type, they'll take your camera away or take your film—because these ceremonies are a part of our life and they have meaning to us. We're the only ones who know their true meaning.

"These people [tourists] come to have a meal and they come for entertainment. They don't understand that this is a part of our religion, a part of our livelihood. And this is the only way that we know how to live and give thanks to our Creator.

"They're trying to make a fast buck off our culture. And I do not like that! I don't like the Indian being exploited in any way!"

Even when visitors aren't trying to make money off the ceremonies, Loretta feels that some exploit Indian culture in another, much more subtle way. "In a way, I think that because so much of the Anglo culture has been lost—because they really don't celebrate religious things in depth, where they actually believe—I think that because they don't have those things anymore, they try to horn in on what we believe and what we partake in."

Christianity has also served to dilute Indian traditions. "It's tough to hold on to them," Loretta admits. "Especially because now we celebrate Christian holidays, such as Christmas." The Catholic Church states that the Creator and the Christian God are one and the same; nevertheless, the perspectives of traditional religion and Christianity differ considerably and, for Loretta, "It's hard trying to tie those two together."

Although her family is Catholic, as she says, "I'm directed toward my Indian, my Native American, religion more than I am to the Catholic religion." Sometimes, Loretta wishes that Pueblo Indians had never accepted Christianity. "Just to see what it would be like," she says wistfully. "But we were kind of forced into it," she adds. "So we didn't have much of a choice."

While Pueblo Indians, like other Native Americans, face great difficulties in keeping their culture intact, they have been the most successful of the North American groups in retaining their identity, traditions, and ceremonies. One result of this is that they attract a lot of attention from tourists. Unlike Loretta, Shawna doesn't think this is a bad thing at all. "No, I don't feel that way," she says. "It's worth it!"

As far as she's concerned, the more attention the better, because it means that others know her people exist. "Just be interested in us," she says. "Be interested in our art work and our pottery work." She's very proud of the fact that so many Pueblo artists have become famous. "Yeah!" she adds enthusiastically. "Because at least they're getting out there and making themselves known."

Like Loretta, Shawna cares very much about her

Shawna Dunlap, age 18

culture. "It's important to us because it's who we are," she says. Thus, Shawna works hard to maintain her traditions. This means dancing at ceremonies, even when she'd rather just watch.

"By dancing, it makes you feel good. It gives you energy," Shawna says. "They say it helps you with your health. But, I don't know, for me, I don't really like dancing," she admits. "I'd rather stand on the sidelines watching everybody, but it's my grandmother—she's into this. She pushes all her grandchildren to dance."

Even though she has to be prodded to get out there, Shawna thinks she'll probably do the same with her own children. "Because I'll know how I was brought up," she explains. "I'll know what it's done for me, and I'll want the same for them."

Shawna plays an important role in the life of her pueblo in another way as well. "I'm the Princess of San Ildefonso Pueblo," she says with pride. "That means that I'm a role model to all the other kids my age and younger. I try to encourage them to get involved in the dances, get involved in the activities that they hold around here."

The princess is elected each year by the council. Being chosen means that the elders in her community feel that she has a solid sense of herself as a person and as a Pueblo Indian. Thus, this is a very high honor.

Part of the strength of the pueblo comes from the fact that everyone knows one another. Therefore, Shawna also tries to get young people to be more visible. "Just get out and show their faces to everybody," she continues. "Because someone like my grandmother, she's always asking, 'Who's that?' They need to come out and show themselves so everybody will know them."

The importance of older people is something most Native Americans agree upon. "We're raised to hold our elders in very high respect," Loretta says. "Because they teach us."

She wishes that younger people of all ethnic groups would recognize how much older people have to offer. "I think that most of the younger generation today do not realize how much knowledge they hold—not just *our* elders but all of them—how much knowledge they hold and how much they can teach you," she adds.

Family is also important to both Loretta and Shawna. But neither one of them has plans to start one of her own yet.

"I say that I'm never going to get married!" Shawna states, laughing. Although she wants to maintain her independence, she likes children and plans to have them. "When I'm older and can financially support them," she adds.

Right now, however, she's preparing to be a god-parent. "It's just like being a parent," she says. "You help them out, teach them, push them to do things they don't want to do." Shawna takes this responsibility seriously and is going to classes to prepare herself for this role.

Loretta has also thought about whether she'll get married or not. In spite of her strong connection to her people and her culture, she thinks she may end up with someone who's not Native American. "I just find myself drawn to people outside my race—maybe it's because I have broadened my horizons more, you know what I'm saying?" she asks. "I've exposed myself to different types of people through going to school in Albuquerque. Right now, the way I think, I probably would marry outside of my race."

"But you never know," she adds. "I might find somebody that I like around here. I'm not going to focus my sights on marrying and finding this Native American man, but you never know—it may happen."

Her sister is married to an Anglo man, so this is not an unusual step for someone in her family. But Jemez women who marry outsiders can't live with their husbands in the pueblo. As Loretta explains, if her sister and her husband were to move back from Missouri, "she could live in Albuquerque, but she couldn't live here with him."

"It's weird, because if a white woman were to marry a man from here, they could live here," Loretta continues. "I think the traditional way is that the woman follows her husband wherever he goes. So I think that's why. Because there's an Anglo woman and a Hispanic woman that live here on the reservation. But they can't witness certain ceremonies," she adds.

Children of mixed couples, regardless of which parent is from Jemez, are considered part of the pueblo, however. "They're part of the tribe," Loretta says. "They can witness whatever, they can take part in whatever."

Although this system may seem unfair to outsiders, Loretta doesn't have a problem with it. "I guess it's just a part of life here," she says. "I never questioned it. I never said, 'Why can't they live here?' Because it just is. If I marry outside the tribe, I would probably be in the same boat."

For Loretta, there are more problematic issues in getting married than whether or not she can continue to live in the pueblo. "Sometimes I think about getting married and having children," she says. "But . . . it's kind of hard for me, because I'm physically handicapped."

Loretta was born with spina bifida, a condition that makes it difficult to walk. Thus, she usually uses a wheelchair or crutches to get around.

In addition to people's perceptions of a handicapped person, Loretta—like Shawna—must deal with the usual tiresome and annoying stereotypes others have of Native Americans.

"They [others] think we're lower than they are," Shawna says. "That we're all poor." But as she points out, there are Native Americans at all economic levels.

"We're just like any other people—we have different people who are rich and not rich."

Even seemingly "flattering" stereotypes—like "all Indians are artistic"—can be offensive, because they lump all people of a group together without regard to who they are as individuals. "It's just like stereotyping black people by saying that all black people can dance," Loretta explains. "Because it's not the case—I personally can't draw anything!"

Many of the other stereotypes she encounters are just plain silly. "When I was in the seventh grade and my sister was in Florida, my brother and I went to visit her, and there were people there who had notions about Native Americans that were just so wild!" Loretta recalls.

"This older man—it freaked me out—he said, 'Do you live in a tipi?' And I said, 'No, do you live in a log cabin?' But they were asking normal questions—they'd just been to too many cowboy and Indian movies."

Over the years, Hollywood has contributed greatly to the spread of misconceptions about Native people. But recently things have been getting better, in large part because Native people have been involved. "I think it's good that more Native Americans are being incorporated into movies or are having input into them," Loretta says.

Still, she thinks there's a lot of room for improvement. "In certain ways they candy-coat things," she continues. "Recently, I saw *Geronimo*. And it was *so* candy-coated. At the end of the movie, they just said he was going to Florida. They didn't tell how he died in a dungeon and they didn't tell how the government broke their promises to him after he surrendered.

"I didn't like that! If you're going to do a movie about somebody's life, why not tell it all even if it makes white people look bad? Because they *did* break their promises, they *did* break treaties, and they *did* treat Indians like scum! Why can't you say it? It's true!"

"The only movie I really, really liked was *Dances with Wolves*," she continues. "Because it was real! I liked the way he—the Anglo man—thought to see the good in Indians. That we're not all savages and heathens and dirty. He saw that Indian people were not what his cavalry and his army made them out to be, that sometimes they were just peaceful on their reservation or wherever they lived, and they just wanted to live how their ancestors lived. And, in fact, the white settlers were being greedy and taking their land.

"And it portrayed how the white man and the Indian could get along. Of course, they were leery at first because he was white and they were Indians, but they got over that and they found they could be the best of friends without these preconceived notions, without other people's influences."

Eliminating preconceived notions and stereotypes of Native Americans is very important to both Loretta and Shawna. As Shawna says simply, "We're just like any other people."

6
MOHAWK

The Mohawk, together with the Oneida, the Onondaga, the Cayuga, the Seneca, and the Tuscarora, form the once powerful Iroquois Confederacy. Originally, the territory of the Confederacy extended from Lake Ontario in the north to Pennsylvania in the south, and from Lake Champlain in the east to the area west of present-day Rochester, New York.

Through a network of alliances with other Native American nations, the Iroquois exerted their influence far beyond these borders and, during the Colonial period, they had political and military control over much of northeastern North America. As allies of the English against the French, they helped to determine which European nation would dominate the history of the continent.

The Iroquois fought in the War of Independence as well, with the Mohawk, Onondaga, Cayuga, and Seneca backing the British and the Oneida and the Tuscarora fighting on the side of the colonists.

Although they were an important influence in the military struggle between European colonizers, the Iroquois talent for political organization played an even more profound role in the shaping of the United States. Their form of government—six separate nations united in a strong democratic confederacy—inspired Benjamin Franklin and others of the Continental Congress, who used the Iroquois Confederacy as a model for uniting thirteen independent colonies into a federation.

As the most eastern of the six Iroquois nations, the Mohawk inhabited the Adirondack Mountains and the northwestern Catskills. Today, their lands have been reduced to five reservations near the border of New York and Canada.

Stacey, TJ, Connie, and David live along the eastern shore of the St. Lawrence River on the Akwesasne Mohawk Reservation (or the St. Regis Indian Reservation, as it is also known). Composed of 29,000 acres, Askwesasne straddles the U.S.–Canadian border, half in the state of New York and half in the provinces of Quebec and Ontario. Of the 9,000 people living at Akwesasne, approximately 5,000 reside on the Canadian side of the reservation and 4,000 on the American side.

Because of the unique location of their reservation, the people of Akwesasne do not have to go through Customs in passing from one side of the border to the other. Moreover, regardless of which side of the reservation they live on, they can go to public school and receive government-funded medical care in either Canada or the United States. However, Mohawks in the Canadian part of Akwesasne are Canadian citizens, while those in New York are American citizens.

The Mohawks consider themselves a separate nation independent of both the United States and Canada, and for those at Akwesasne their identity as Mohawks is what matters. Thus, they, like other Iroquois nations, prefer to be called North American—not Canadian or American—Native Americans. As Connie's mother puts it, "We try not to look at it like American and Canadian, because it's one reservation. What we all try to do—the American and the Canadian tribal councils—is live together as one."

AKWESASNE MOHAWK RESERVATION
(ST. REGIS INDIAN RESERVATION)
HOGANSBURG, NEW YORK

We're no different from any other race. —*TJ*

That pretty much sums it up. —*Connie*

In addition to territory on the mainland of the United States and Canada, Akwesasne also includes nearby Cornwall Island in the St. Lawrence River. Stacey lives on this island with her mother, her stepfather, her brother, her two stepbrothers, her half brother, and a number of four-legged friends.

"I'm the one in the family with all the animals," she says. "I have two horses—well, one's a horse and the other one's a pony—and I have a dog and a cat. My mother bought the pony for Joe [her little brother] but he never took care of it, so she gave it to me." Stacey was willing to take on the responsibility. "You've got to go down there every day and take care of them, feed them grain," she explains. "We've got a lot of room in the pasture, so they just eat the grass."

Like Fawn, Stacey does beadwork as a way of earning money. "We have a girl selling our beadwork in Cornwall," she says. "My mom makes the barrettes, I make the necklaces. I'm starting to get into rings now, beaded rings. And I make quite a few of these," Stacey adds, pointing to delicate beaded webs called dreamcatchers. These webs are hung in homes to protect sleeping people against bad dreams. Good dreams can pass through the tiny hole at the center of the dreamcatcher, but bad dreams are trapped in the web where they are destroyed by the light of dawn.

Connie and TJ, who've been going together for five months now, met each other through Stacey. "I have a friend, Stacey, and she lives on Cornwall Island," Connie recalls. "I went to her house, and there he was."

As Connie explains, "I didn't really get to know him then. But one day, I called him long distance. We talked for two hours. Then I got home and he called me and we talked for ten hours!"

"We were just talking about ourselves, getting to know each other better," TJ adds. "Just taking our time, talking about things." Fortunately for their parents' wallets, they usually talk to each other in person now.

David has less free time to hang out than Stacey, Connie, and TJ. His parents own a successful Mexican restaurant in the town of Cornwall and—like the rest of his family—David has been part of the staff since it opened over three years ago. "After school, I make the guacamole and wash dishes," he says. He likes working in the restaurant and is proud of his contribution. "I was here with it when it started out," he says with a smile. "And now it's doing good!"

Although all four of these young people live in the Canadian part of the reservation, they can choose to go

Stacey Montour, age 13

to school in the United States if they wish. Elementary- and middle-school children in Akwesasne have their choice of the Mohawk school on Cornwall Island or the local public schools in Canada or the United States. When they reach high school, they can go to either the Canadian high school in the area or the nearby American high school. Most kids go to the school that is closest to them.

TJ goes to the Mohawk school, and he likes it a lot. Although it's in Canada, some of the courses are different from those in other Canadian schools. "We don't have French," TJ explains. "We just have Mohawk every day." Because it's also a Catholic school, the Mohawk school teaches Catholicism as well. However, students who aren't Catholic—such as those of the traditional Longhouse religion, the Assembly of God, or other Protestant denominations—are excused from class.

Stacey and Connie are members of the Assembly of God, but David and TJ come from Catholic families. Historically, the Catholic church has been a major force in this part of Canada and has had a strong influence on the lives of many Indians here. Only a generation ago, the church told Catholic Mohawks that they jeopardized their souls if they participated in Native American dances or associated with "pagans" of the Longhouse religion.

Fortunately, this has changed. Native people who are Catholic, as well as those of other Christian denominations, have realized the importance of incorporating their Native American traditions and spirituality into their lives. Thus, unlike their parents, young people today no longer feel they have to choose between being a Mohawk and being a Christian.

Like TJ, Stacey has been going to the Mohawk school, where the Mohawk language is her favorite subject. "It's probably the best subject that I have," she says.

Richard (TJ) Point, age 14

Although she isn't fluent yet, she can generally get a sense of what people are talking about when they speak in Mohawk.

The school goes only to the eighth grade, so next year Stacey will be attending the regular public high school in Cornwall. She worries a little about what this will be like. "I think it's going to be all right," she says, hopefully. "Because you get to meet a lot of people."

On the other hand, she's somewhat concerned about how these new people will treat her. "I know some of them are against us," Stacey says. "They call us wagon burners. They're scared of us, I guess, because a long time ago, we used to scalp people . . . they're scared of us because of that."

David will be going to high school on the Canadian side next year as well, but he seems more comfortable with the idea. His sisters, as well as his father, went to the same school, and he feels it will be OK.

Up until now, Connie has been going to Salmon River school in New York. "Indians and whites—most of them—they get along," she says of her experience there. "But some of the Indian kids, they get treated differently. Some teachers don't like Indian kids. But there's quite a few Indians [in Salmon River school]," she adds, "so it's not that bad for me."

Soon, however, she'll be moving on to an American high school and, like Stacey, she's nervous about what it will be like. "I heard it's going to be hard at Messena," she says. "My friends said that some of the white people don't like Indians. They say it's not that bad, but . . ." She expects that there may be some fights, and she isn't much of a fighter. "I probably can be, though!" she adds.

Stacey, Connie, David, and TJ all think that many white kids see them in a negative way, and this hurts and angers them. "People over there don't know that we're almost the same," TJ says. "They think we're a

Connie Oakes, age 15

lot different than they are. We're supposed to be dressed up in feathers, you know."

"They probably think we're really mean," Connie adds. "But we're not bad people!"

When you don't feel welcome, it's harder to like school and to do well. Whether this is part of the reason or not, many young people in Akwesasne don't finish high school. "I know a lot of kids around here —teenagers—who have already quit school," Stacey says. Her brother and his friend are the only two left in their group of friends who are still in school. "I hope they stay!" she says.

Those who do finish often wait before going to college. "Usually they take a year off from school and figure out what they want to do," Stacey continues. "Then they join college or go wherever . . . or they just quit school from there."

Stacey definitely plans to graduate. "And I'm going to go to college!" she says emphatically. "I told my mother that I'm not going to get married. . . . Well, I'll probably get married eventually, but I'm not going to start a family until I get out of college, so nothing will stop me from going."

She isn't sure what she wants to study, however. With her love of animals, being a vet might seem a logical choice, but as Stacey explains, "I was thinking about that, but I'm not sure. I'm softhearted, and if an animal dies in front of me . . .

"My mother wants me to be a nurse, but I'm not too interested in that," Stacey continues. "I like crafts. They tested us in school to see what we wanted to be, and they found that I was really interested in doing crafts."

They also suggested that she might like building things. This appealed to her as well. "My father is an engineer. He builds houses and a bunch of things. He's a carpenter too. And my mom, she insulates houses,"

Stacey explains. "And so I was thinking maybe I'd do something like that."

David plans to go to college too, but he wants to be a lawyer. "Money!" he replies, when asked why he's chosen that career. "And it's fun," he adds.

David's on the honor roll at school, so he should do well in law school. Plus, he's already had some courtroom experience. Recently, as part of a class project, David was the defense lawyer in a mock trial. "We won!" he says, smiling.

Like many kids her age, Connie isn't sure what she wants to do after school. TJ, however, has firm plans. "I'm going into professional sports," he says. His grandfather has been urging him to be a baseball pitcher because that's where the most money is, but, as TJ says, "I can't even throw a ball." He is good at football, though, so that's the sport he's concentrating on.

David, Connie, and TJ haven't given much thought to where they want to live after school. But Stacey thinks she'd like to return to Akwesasne. There are several things that would draw her back. "The quiet," she says. "All the memories."

Things have been changing on the reservation, however, and this concerns her. "Well, sometimes now, I notice that there are kids who are really getting out of hand," she says. "Some people are getting into drugs a lot. It never was a problem, but now it's getting bad. I know a lot of close relatives that are into it," she continues. "I'm worried about them, what's going to happen."

Although the relationship between white kids and Indians isn't always that great, many Mohawk and whites do date. "My brother was going out with a person who's not Mohawk," Stacey says. "And a lot of guys are dating people who aren't Mohawk."

But the consequences of marrying a non-Mohawk are different for a girl than for a boy, and that influences how Stacey feels about possibly falling in love with someone from outside her community.

"If I meet a guy that I really like, I don't care what he is, as long as I'm really interested," she says. "But I've been hearing stuff that if I marry a white person, I'll get kicked off the reservation. For the Indian girls, if they marry a white person, the girls would get kicked off. But if it's the Indian guys that marry a white girl, the white girls get to come on the reservation."

Stacey isn't sure of the reason for this policy. But it's a high price to pay, and it doesn't seem right to her. "I don't think it's fair to be treated that way," she comments. Thus, while she's open to being with someone from any race as long as it's a guy she really likes, Stacey hopes that guy turns out to be another Mohawk.

At her age, though, most kids on the reservation hang around in groups, rather than pairing off. And they spend their free time the way kids all over the country do. "We goof off," says TJ, laughing.

"We usually go to see a movie, go swimming. Or we just hang around somebody's house, invite a lot of friends up there to come over and talk," Stacey adds.

Sports are a big activity for everybody. "I play soccer, volleyball, basketball," David says. These are Connie's favorite sports too. "And there's other things," she adds, "like lacrosse, swimming, and everything."

There's also a race called the long run. "The kids, they make their own track," Stacey says. "About two miles long. And they get prizes for coming in first, second, and third."

Since the reservation is located on the St. Lawrence River, it's no surprise that swimming is so popular. But the waters around Cornwall Island may have an unusual inhabitant. "Some people have been saying they've been seeing something in the water," says Stacey. "They say it's pretty big."

Recently, a girl and her mother claimed to have seen the creature. "They said it looked like a log, because it was real still and it was long," Stacey continues. "It came up a little bit and she [the girl] saw eyes. Her mother looked over there and, when they saw it, it went back under."

Although the idea of a mysterious creature in the river may seem far-fetched, others have reported seeing the animal as well. The Mohawk have taken these reports seriously enough to send divers underwater to see what's there. "The divers, they went under and found big tunnels under the island," Stacey says.

While this is kind of spooky, the creature hasn't done anything to anyone and doesn't seem to be harmful. So it hasn't taken the fun out of going in the water. "When you're swimming, you're having so much fun, you really don't think about it," Stacey says. "But later on, it comes to you, and you think, 'Let's get out!'" Still, she'd really like to see it someday.

Mohawk cultural activities are also fun. Stacey has been dancing since she was young, and feels it's an important part of her. "Sometimes we have practice after school," she says. "Here at the school, we have our native dancing and quite a few people come from other places to watch. We travel too—to Tyendinaga [a Mohawk reservation on the Canadian shore of Lake Ontario]."

She also enjoys powwows. "There was a powwow in Ottowa. It was really big!" she says. "They had stands selling beadwork. Some people even brought their tents and everything, and they spent two nights there."

David goes to powwows too. Last year his family went to the biggest powwow of all, the Gathering of Nations in Albuquerque, New Mexico. For David and his family, being a part of a group of 70,000 Native Americans was a powerful emotional experience.

There were 1,600 dancers on the floor at one time.

David Papineau, age 13

"They just kept going out on the floor," David said. "They couldn't move anymore, so they just stood there and danced."

Although he liked watching others dance, he was too shy to get out there himself, at least in such a big crowd. "He wouldn't dance with me!" his father says. "They were doing the buck dance. I wanted to dance and I tried to get him up." David laughs when his father jokingly accuses him of doing the chicken dance instead.

Both TJ and Connie like Native American songs and dancing. "Every weekend in school, we have Indian dances where kids dance and sing for about an hour," TJ says. Connie goes to another school, though, and she doesn't have the same opportunities to do this.

"I used to dance in school," she says, "But then I went to Salmon River. Once in a while a Native Indian speaker would come and dance for us, but I haven't been dancing lately." This bothers her a lot. "I'm almost losing it," she sighs. For TJ and Connie, dancing and their language are among the most important parts of their culture, and they don't want to lose either one.

Native Americans are often in the position of having to juggle the demands of two different worlds. They work hard to maintain their own culture, but at the same time, they have to be able to get along in the larger, non-Indian world. With Akwesasne and their lives split between the United States and Canada, Stacey, David, Connie, and TJ must try even harder to maintain their identity as Mohawks. But they're determined to succeed!

Like the young people presented in this book, Native American teens throughout the country struggle to be themselves and to have others understand and appreciate who they are. If the teenagers from the Mohawk, Anishnabe, Quinault, Shinnecock, Cherokee, and Pueblo

peoples are any indication, Native American adolescents are more than willing and able to express their
thoughts, feelings, and concerns. It's up to the rest of
us to listen.

◆◆◆◆◆◆◆◆◆◆◆◆◆◆◆◆◆◆◆◆◆◆◆◆◆◆◆◆◆◆◆◆◆◆◆

ATTENDING POWWOWS, FEASTS, AND DANCES

Powwows, Pueblo feast days, and many ceremonial dances are open to everyone, not just Native Americans. Native people welcome others to these gatherings for several reasons. First, they are proud of their culture and want others to understand and appreciate who they are. Inviting non-Native people to participate in these events is one way of helping others learn about Native Americans. In addition, many Native artists sell the things they produce at powwows and benefit from being able to introduce their work to the larger community. But most important, Native Americans are, as they have always been, a generous people willing to include others and to share what they know with them.

Powwows are a lot of fun for everyone! But in addition to being social events, they are also important religious occasions. Thus, people who attend are expected to behave respectfully.

This means that taking videos or photographs of dances or recording the drumming or singing may be prohibited. There will be signs or announcements to that effect if this is the case. It's a good idea to take these warnings seriously! Understandably, Native people become very offended when these restrictions are disregarded, and those who disobey the rules can have their film or cameras confiscated.

There are powwows in virtually every state. A calendar of these events can be purchased from:

The Book Publishing Company
P.O. Box 99
Summertown, TN 38483
1-800-695-2241

In addition, the Indian Pueblo Cultural Center publishes a free calendar of traditional Indian dances held at pueblos in New Mexico. This calendar can be obtained by writing to:

Indian Pueblo Cultural Center
2401 Twelfth Street, NW
Albuquerque, NM 87102
(505) 843-7270

◆◆◆◆◆◆◆◆◆◆◆◆◆◆◆◆◆◆◆◆◆◆◆◆◆◆◆◆◆◆◆◆◆◆◆◆◆

FURTHER READING

As a look at any library listing illustrates, a great number of books about Native Americans have been written. Most of these books are good. Unfortunately, a few still perpetuate stereotypes and misinformation about Native people.

Therefore, use your judgment when reading books about Native Americans. If you have the feeling that the author is putting down Indians, even subtly, or seems surprised when mentioning their accomplishments, take the book back to the library or bookstore where you got it. It's not worth reading.

There are some guidelines you can use to determine whether a book is likely to be worthwhile before you bring it home. One of the best ways is to choose books written by Native Americans themselves. One such book is *Land of the Quinault*, edited by Pauline K. Capoeman and published by the Quinault Indian Nation, Taholah, Washington 98587.

After reading about the drama *Unto These Hills*, you may want to learn more about the forced removal of the Cherokee, Choctaw, Chicksasaw, Creek, and Serminole people from the southeastern United States. *And Still the Waters Run: The Betrayal of the Five Civilized Tribes* by Angie Debo (Princeton University Press; 1940, 1991) details this story, providing quotes from Indians who actually lived through it.

Atlas of the North American Indian, by Carl Waldman (New York: Facts on File, 1985), is very good and has detailed maps of events in the history of Native Americans. In addition, it lists all the federal and state reservations in the United States.

There are many spectacular collections of photographs of Native American people. Perhaps the best-known photographer of North American Indians was Edward S. Curtis, who photographed western tribes from the very late 1890s to the early 1900s, when their cultures were still relatively intact. A book of his pictures, *Native Nations* has recently been published by Little, Brown and Company (Boston: 1993) and is definitely worth looking at.

Another beautifully illustrated book with an interesting and easily readable text is *Indian Tribes of North America*, by Josepha Sherman (New York: Portland House, 1990). This book contains paintings and photographs of Native Americans from the earliest times of European contact to today, including some very good pictures of present-day Mohawk, Ojibway, Cherokee, and San Ildefonso people.

Native Americans are now writing fiction as well. In addition to offering good stories, these books provide an idea of what it is like to be a Native person today. Perhaps the best known of these new writers is Louise Erdrich. Three of her books are *The Beet Queen*, *Love Medicine*, and *Tracks*.

N. Scott Momaday's books include *House Made of Dawn* (New York: HarperCollins, 1989) and *The Ancient Child* (New York: HarperCollins, 1990). Another very good Native American poet and storyteller is Leslie Marmon Silko, who wrote *Storyteller* (New York: Arcade Publishing, 1981).

Finally, in a category all by itself is *Black Elk Speaks*, as told by John G. Neihardt (Lincoln, Nebraska: University of Nebraska Press, 1979). Originally published in 1932, it presents the life and thoughts of an Oglala Sioux holy man who lived through the massacre at Wounded Knee.

INDEX

Adobe homes, 87
African-Americans and
    Shinnecocks, 44–46
Aiyana, 44–50
Akwesasne Mohawk Re-
    servation, 107–120
Alcohol use, 39, 48, 60–61,
    81, 83–84
Anasazi people, 87
Anishnabe people, 51–71
Artistic traditions
    Anishnabes, 67, 68–69
    Cherokees, 22–23
    Mohawks, 108
    Pueblo people, 93–94, 97
    Quinaults, 76
*Atlas of the North American
    Indian* (Waldman), 123

Basketweaving, 22–23, 47
Bay Mills Indian Reserva-
    tion, 53–71
Beadwork, 108
Benton, Ginew. *See*
    Ginew
Bering Strait, 49
Birch trees, 51
Black Elk Speaks (Nei-
    hardt), 124
Black, Lolita. *See* Lolita
Black, Stanley. *See* Stanley

Book Publishing Com-
    pany, 121
Books about Native Ameri-
    cans, 123–125
Boredom, 61, 81–82, 92
Bradley, Matthew. *See*
    Matthew
Business, starting a, 94–95,
    108

Cajero, Loretta. *See* Loretta
Cameron, Fawn. *See* Fawn
Ceremonies, Native. *See*
    Culture, Native Ameri-
    can
Cherokee people, 13–41
Chippewas. *See* Anishnabe
    people
Christianity, 41, 70–71, 97,
    110
Clamming, 66
Coming of Age Ceremony,
    69–71
Competition, 35, 68
Conflicting obligations,
    95–96, 97, 119
Connie, 106–120
Culture, Native American
    Anishnabes, 55–56, 69–
    71
    Cherokees, 26–28

Culture, Native American
   (continued)
   Mohawks, 117, 119, 121–
      122
   powwows and dancing,
      10–11
   Pueblo people, 95–97, 99
   Quinaults, 84–86
   Shinnecocks, 44, 47–48

Dances With Wolves, 28, 63,
   103
Dancing, 10–11, 47, 55–56,
   69, 84–85, 117, 119,
   121–122
David, 106–120
De Soto, Hernando, 13
Diseases that accompanied
   whites, 73
Drug use, 39, 48, 61, 81–84
Dunlap, Shawna. *See*
   Shawna

Economic entitlements,
   36–37, 77
Education
   Anishnabes, 61, 67–68
   Cherokees, 35–38
   Mohawks, 110, 112, 114–
      115
   Pueblo people, 90, 94–
      95
   Quinaults, 77, 80, 82
   Shinnecocks, 48–49
Emerson, 13–41
Entertainment, lack of, 61,
   81–82, 92

Erdrich, Louise, 124
Europeans, 51–52, 73, 87
Exploitation of cultural
   events, White, 96–97

Fancy dancing, 11
Fawn, 51–71
Fishing, 82–83
Future, looking toward
   the, 37–38, 48–49, 82,
   85–86, 114–115

Gathering of Nations, 117,
   119
Geronimo, 102
Ginew, 51–71
Grass dancer, 69

Hunting, 67

Ignorance about Native
   Americans, 18, 20, 64,
   83
Indian Pueblo Cultural
   Center, 122
*Indian Tribes of North
   America* (Sherman),
   124
Iroquois Confederacy, 105

Jackson, Andrew, 13
Jemez Pueblo, 89–103
Jewelry, 56, 58
Johnson, Shondi. *See*
   Shondi
Jumper, Winnie. *See*
   Winnie

Kristy, 51–71

Land, attempts at taking
    Native Americans', 67
Land of the Quinault
    (Capoeman), 123
Language, 22, 23, 110, 112
Last of the Mohicans, The,
    28
LeBlanc, Kristy. *See* Kristy
Legends, 23, 24, 84, 85, 117
Little People, Cherokee's,
    24
Lolita, 74–86
Loretta, 88–103

Marriage between non-
    Native and Native
    Americans
    Anishnabes, 62
    Cherokees, 20, 27
    Mohawks, 115–116
    Pueblo people, 100–101
Marriages among different
    Native tribes, 74
Matthew, 13–41
McCoy, Skooter. *See*
    Skooter
Media's portrayal of Na-
    tive Americans, 28–32,
    62–64, 102–103
Medicine, 23, 47
Membership criteria, 20–
    21, 28–29
Mohawk people, 105–120
Momaday, N. Scott, 26, 124
Montour, Stacey. *See* Stacey

Native American Youth
    Organization (NAYO),
    33
Native Nations (Curtis),
    124
Nature, being close to,
    46–47, 71
New Mexico, 89–90
Northwest Coastal style of
    drawing, 76

Oakes, Connie. *See*
    Connie
Ojibway people. *See*
    Anishnabe people
Older people, attitudes
    toward, 60, 99–100

Papineau, David. *See*
    David
Point, Richard (TJ). *See* TJ
Potlatches, 85
Pottery, 93–94
Powwows, 10–11, 47,
    55–56, 117, 119, 121–
    122
Pregnant teens, 77–80
Pueblo people, 87–103

Quileute tribe, 74
Quinault Nation Indian
    Dancers, 84
Quinault people, 73–86

Racism, 36–37, 58–59, 101–
    102, 112, 114
Removal, the, 13

Reservation life, 38–40, 48, 60, 66, 116
Roseau River Indian Reservation, 53–71

San Ildefonso Pueblo, 89–103
Scrubs, 47
Sequoya, 22
Shawna, 87–103
Shinnecock people, 41–50
Shondi, 13–41
Skin color and relations between Native Americans, 27
Skooter, 13–41
Smith, Aiyana. See Aiyana
Sports, 32–33, 35, 80–81, 81, 116
St. Regis Indian Reservation, 107–120
Stacey, 106–120
Stanley, 74–86

Stereotypes, 83, 101–102
Storytelling, 23–24
Sweat lodge, 47–48

Teenage and Pregnancy, Parenting, Prevention Program (TAPPP), 78, 80
Thunderheart, 63
TJ, 106–120
Tourism, 29, 32, 96
Traditional dancing, 11
Trees, replanting, 83

Unto These Hills, 29, 31–32, 123

War of Independence, 105
Welch, Emerson. See Emerson
Wickiups, 66–67
Wigwams, 41
Winnie, 13–41